Savor the Memories

Marguerite Marceau Henderson

Savor the Memories

Copyright © 2002
Marguerite Marceau Henderson
1529 Hubbard Avenue
Salt Lake City, Utah
801-582-9204

Library of Congress Number:
ISBN: 0-9714942-0-7

Designed, Edited, and Manufactured by
Favorite Recipes® Press
An imprint of

FRP.

P. O. Box 305142
Nashville, Tennessee 37230
1-800-358-0560

Art Director: Steve Newman
Designer: Starletta Polster
Project Manager: Susan Larson

Manufactured in the United States of America
First Printing: 2002   6,000 copies

Acknowledgements

There have been many people whose paths have crossed mine during my twenty- plus years in the culinary field. First and foremost, thanks to Eileen Mullane, my friend, confidante, business partner, and official recipe and martini taster. We have been through it all together, from the inception of two successful businesses, deaths, marriages, graduations of our children, and all that life has handed to us. Eileen, your spunky Irish spirit kept it together.

Thanks to our loyal customers who believed in our entrepreneurial spirit. You kept coming back for more and we were glad. Thanks to my cooking students, many of whom are now my good friends. Your desire for more knowledge has kept my love of food alive, and you continue to inspire me. Let's have another twenty years of fun in the kitchen.

Thanks to the staff at Cucina, some of whom have been there since the doors first opened in October 1995. We could not have been such a success without your tireless enthusiasm. Over the years I have had the pleasure of working with some of the best chefs and most talented cooks in Utah. Thanks to all the "people in the back," the kitchen staff, for it is your love of food and your creativity that keep the customers happy. It was an honor to work with such talent. You made it a joy to come to work every day.

Thanks to Ellen Hutchinson, my good friend of thirty-five years. You are a true artist. We share the love of good food, good art, good wine, and good theater. Trips to New York would not be complete without dinner and a show with Ellen. You and your art are inspirational.

Thanks to my brother, George Marceau, and his wife, Maria. You cared for our mother in her final years. You nurtured her, fed her, and made her comfortable in her final days. You are saints.

Thanks to all my cherished friends, family, neighbors, and supporters. For years you have been there for me, given me words of encouragement and love, and hours of advice. You are my biggest fans, my cheerleaders, and my champions. You know who you are.

And finally, thanks to my husband, Robert, and my two children, Justin Churchill Henderson and Sarah Elizabeth Henderson. You have been there during the early catering days, helping in the kitchen. You have been there for the opening of two stores, helping wherever you could. And you have been there helping to create memories for the family during the holidays, celebrations, or while just enjoying dinners around the kitchen table at night. Justin and Sarah, I hope the love of food and family will live on in your future families. You two are the joys of our lives.

Dedication

This book is dedicated to the memory of my mother, Rose Filippi Marceau. She was my guiding light, my conscience, and my influence in all that is in good taste and tastes good. She had her own style—a timeless style. She cooked with the freshest ingredients from the local vegetable markets, the butcher shops, the seafood stores, the Italian salumerias, and the bakeries in Brooklyn and Manhattan. She would scour specialty food stores for the exact cinnamon oil for her ricotta cake filling, she would walk miles to purchase fresh ravioli at the pasta store, and then she would go to buy the appropriate wines to serve with each meal.

Rose Filippi Marceau

This cookbook has been put on the back burner for many years due to other business commitments. This year, 2002, was the year I was determined to get it published. The impetus was the death of my mother, Rose. After suffering for many years with Alzheimer's disease, she died peacefully in the spring of 2001.

Rose, or Grandma Rose as everyone knew her, was born in Sicily in 1915. She immigrated to America in 1920 with her family. They settled in Brooklyn, New York, where she lived for most of her life and where I was born and raised. Rose was a lover of everything beautiful: food, flowers, table settings, décor, and clothes. She was a special person—giving, loving, and grateful for her two children and four grandchildren. We, in turn, were grateful for her. It was my mother who taught me to cook. I literally learned at her apron strings in her kitchen in Brooklyn. She taught me that food was to be revered, with no shortcuts, no skimping on the best ingredients—just good, honest, fresh ingredients, presented simply but elegantly.

Grandma Rose's food was inspirational. Her creamy lemon rice pudding with a hint of cinnamon was ethereal. Her tomato sauce, simmering on the stove on Sunday mornings while we went to mass, was seasoned perfectly. She loved to try new recipes from the *New York Times* or from a friend or neighbor. Guests at her home, whether for Sunday dinner or for cake and coffee, were treated to her easy style of entertainment. Her table was set with fine china and silver and adorned with fresh flowers from the garden. Her Thanksgiving dinners were legendary, starting with antipasto, then pasta, turkey, stuffing, vegetables, salad, and, of course, pies, cakes, cannoli, espresso, and liqueurs.

My brother George and I carry on our mother's memory with our love of food and wine. The night before my mother's funeral this past spring, my brother hosted a dinner for about twenty relatives in his home in upstate New York. We shared stories about Grandma Rose. We shared her fine recipes. We laughed, we cried, and we toasted my mother's memory. She would have been proud of her legacy and would have loved to have been at that dinner, reveling in the celebration of family, food, and tradition. I hope I have instilled this love of the Italian tradition of family and food in my two children, so that they, too, can savor the memories.

Thank you, Mom. You made me who I am, and you were a model for who I hope to be.

Preface

Cucina opened in the fall of 1995 in Salt Lake's "Avenues" area, a neighborhood dotted with old Victorian homes and mansions. We were a hit from day one, a great addition to a franchise-infested city that seemed to have forgotten the virtues of small businesses. Within a few years, various publications had bestowed upon us awards such as "Best Take-out," "Best Caterer," "Best Clandestine Coffee Stop," "Best Neighborhood Joint," and, in the prestigious *Zagat's Guide to Utah*, "Best Meal Deal" and "Best Deli in Utah." Our food was recently rated twenty-three out of thirty. Not bad for a little gourmet deli in Salt Lake City.

My business partner and good friend, Eileen Mullane, and I worked long and hard to establish Cucina as a fine neighborhood establishment. Like many entrepreneurs, we have cried at our failures more times than we want to recall and have rejoiced at our many successes. We have made our mark in Salt Lake City. Cucina, we feel, paved the way for other small businesses in our neighborhood and is thriving more than we ever thought it could, thanks to our loyal customers and their support.

As the restaurant grew, so did the repertoire of recipes we prepared daily. Our friendly customers would ask if certain recipes were available to the public, and we gladly handed out our little secrets. After years in the kitchen of Cucina, I began to teach cooking classes once again. It was a pleasure to impart my knowledge of food, wine, technique, and hints for easy entertaining and preparation to my students. I love to share the joy of food, and I know my enthusiasm is contagious. I have some students who have taken my classes for over twenty years! As a caterer before opening Cucina, and also catering through the restaurant, I developed tantalizing yet easy recipes for the home chef. So, it was inevitable that over the years I was asked, "When are you going to write a cookbook with recipes from Cucina, your cooking classes, your television appearances, and from your home kitchen?" Well, the time is now, and here it is.

This book is dotted with little anecdotes for some of the recipes. They light a spark in me, the stories make me laugh, they make me reminisce of days past, and they make me want to share them with you, the reader. Enjoy *Savor the Memories,* read it, use it, and hopefully it will become part of your life, too.

CUCINA
A GOURMET DELI

Introduction

This book was written with the everyday cook in mind. It is to be used as a guide for those who enjoy good food, easy preparation of food, and using recipes that are tried and true.

The philosophy of *Savor the Memories* is to create a lasting impression with food for those you love, to cherish traditions in your life with family and friends, and to cook with confidence that each and every dish will please your guests.

The freshest ingredients are extremely important. I have kept the diversity of the Mediterranean kitchen in mind when creating these recipes and have made allowances for product availability. Follow this simple rule: Use the best products available to you, the freshest ingredients available to you, and use the simplest processes to create inspirational dishes from your kitchen.

Recipes should be used as a springboard. They are meant to stimulate your imagination, stimulate your taste buds, and stimulate the creative juices in the cook.

Simply stated, food should be prepared without trepidation. The unifying factors in all the recipes in this book are their simplicity, their freshness, their taste, and their history in my family and my career.

Buon appetito!

Table of Contents

Tips and Hints for Entertaining from Marguerite's Kitchen

1. Use kosher salt on lamb, pork or beef roasts, roasted chicken, or grilled meats. The coarseness give the outer surface some texture and the salt does not extract any of the juices of the meats.

2. Sauté onions first for several minutes in butter or oil before adding garlic. Since onions always take longer to cook, the garlic won't burn.

3. Always add 1 tablespoon of salt and 1 tablespoon of oil to a pot of boiling water when making pasta, and always use at least 4 quarts of water per pound of pasta.

4. Line your cheese and fruit trays with fresh grape or fig leaves from your garden. Use fresh, edible flowers from your garden as garnish for any platter.

5. Tie a piece of colorful ribbon around the stem of a cluster of grapes to enhance a fruit tray. Make little "bouquets" of fresh herbs, tied with colorful thin ribbons, to garnish your trays.

6. Sprinkle powdered sugar and place mint sprigs on any dessert which needs a pick-me-up—such as chocolate cakes, bread puddings, pies, cobblers, etc.

7. Use martini glasses, goblets, colored wine glasses, etc., to hold salsas, dips, and sauces for added dimension to your table.

8. Use what's available all year-round from the garden to enhance your dining table, such as fruit blossoms in spring, grape and fig leaves in summer, colorful autumn leaves in fall, and pine boughs in winter. What looks ordinary on a tree might look completely different surrounding your platters.

9. When planning menus for your parties, remember to keep the menu simple and within your expertise. One fabulous dish done to perfection will always outshine four mediocre ones, and your guests will recall that one special presentation.

10. Use fresh seasonal foods simply prepared. Shop the farmer's markets, the local butchers, the artisan bakeries, the neighborhood gourmet shop. Remember, the small business people will spark your imagination. They are your best friends when it comes to quality and consistency.

11. Garnish, garnish, garnish…a single pansy, a fresh thyme sprig, a cinnamon stick, a perfect rose, a branch of ivy, a long strand of citrus zest turned into a "ribbon." That extra touch shows your guests that you really want to make them happy.

12. Serve your food on platters of various shapes and sizes. Use square plates, oval platters, and rectangular trays and remember height. Tall cake stands are perfect cheese platters, clear vases make the ideal breadstick holders, etc. Use larger trays rather than smaller ones. Food always looks better "big," not crowded.

13. Always keep an eye out for that one perfect "sale" item—one imported napkin to line a bread basket, the one little bowl for olives or nuts, two odd goblets to hold salsa or sauces, and the mismatched platter for a wedge of cheese and a cluster of Champagne grapes.

14. For dinner parties of six or more, serve family style. It keeps the conversation flowing, the guests are more relaxed, and they can determine their own portion size.

15. My rule of thumb for entertaining: mix, match, and have fun. Use color, texture, style, and, most of all, sit back and savor the memories.

Appetizers

*Savor the Memories of my aunts, uncles, and cousins
gathering for Thanksgiving or Sunday Dinners...
sipping wine, eating celery sticks stuffed with
Roquefort and cream cheese mixture topped with a sprinkle
of paprika on my mother's green Depression glass platter.*

Garlic Basil White Bean Dip with Crostini

2	cups cannellini or white northern beans (15-ounce can), drained	1/2	teaspoon salt
1	tablespoon minced garlic	1/8	teaspoon white pepper
2	tablespoons chopped fresh basil	1/4	cup olive oil

Garnish

1	tablespoon olive oil	1	tablespoon chopped fresh basil

Place beans, garlic, basil, salt and pepper in food processor. Purée for 30 seconds. Slowly add the olive oil. Purée for another minute or until mixture is smooth. Transfer to a bowl, drizzle with a little more olive oil, sprinkle with chopped fresh basil for garnish and serve with Crostini (toasted bread rounds) or breadsticks.

Makes about 2 cups

Crostini

1	pound loaf Italian or French baguette, cut into 1/4-inch thick slices	1/4	cup olive oil
		1	tablespoon minced garlic

Place bread slices on baking sheet large enough to hold them in a single layer. In a small bowl, combine the oil and garlic. Brush tops of bread with oil mixture. Bake in preheated 400-degree oven for 5 minutes or until golden. Turn over the bread slices and brush with more olive oil. Bake another 3 to 5 minutes or until golden. Can be made ahead, secured in an airtight bag after allowed to cool.

Makes about 24 crostini

Hot Crab Meat and Artichoke Dip

1/2	cup mayonnaise		4	to 5 drops Tabasco sauce
1/2	cup sour cream		1	cup shredded Romano or Parmesan cheese
4	ounces cream cheese, softened			
1/4	cup chopped red onion		1/2	pound flaked crab meat
1/4	cup chopped parsley			15-ounce can artichoke hearts, drained and coarsely chopped
2	tablespoons horseradish			

In a bowl, combine the mayonnaise, sour cream, cream cheese, onion, parsley, horseradish, Tabasco and Romano cheese. Mix well. Gently stir in the crab meat and artichokes, and pour into a 2-quart baking or soufflé dish. (Can be made ahead up to this point.) Bake, covered, for 20 minutes in a 350-degree oven; remove cover and bake 5 additional minutes. Serve at once with crackers, crostini or crudités.

Makes 8 to 10 servings

Caponata (Sicilian Eggplant Appetizer)

1/2	cup olive oil		1/2	cup pitted kalamata olives
2	medium eggplants, cut into 1-inch cubes		2	tablespoons capers
			1	tablespoon anchovy paste or 2 anchovy fillets
1	onion, diced			
2	tablespoons minced garlic		1/2	cup red wine vinegar
4	ribs celery, sliced thinly on diagonal		1	tablespoon dried oregano
1	green pepper, cored and diced		2	tablespoons sugar
2	cups diced Italian tomatoes in juices		1	teaspoon salt
1	cup sliced green olives with pimientos		1/2	teaspoon ground black pepper

In medium saucepan, heat olive oil. Add the eggplant and sauté until soft, about 5 minutes, stirring often. Add onion. Cook another minute. Add the garlic, celery and green pepper. Cook on low heat for another 3 minutes. Add tomatoes, olives, capers, anchovy paste, vinegar, oregano, sugar, salt and pepper. Cover; simmer for 20 minutes. Taste for seasoning. Cool to room temperature, then refrigerate.

Makes 4 cups

Note: This dish tastes best made a day ahead to allow flavors to mellow. It is wonderful served hot on pasta or grilled fish or chicken. It can also be served at room temperature as part of an antipasto platter.

Warmed Goat Cheese with Sun-Dried Tomatoes

8-ounce log goat cheese
1/4 cup julienne-cut sun-dried tomatoes, rehydrated in hot water
1/4 cup olive oil
1 tablespoon minced garlic
2 large roasted red peppers, cut into thin strips
1/4 cup pitted kalamata olives
1/4 cup toasted pine nuts
2 sprigs of fresh rosemary or thyme
1 recipe Crostini (page 12)

Place goat cheese log in a decorative 12-inch diameter baking dish. Place rehydrated sun-dried tomatoes in a small bowl with oil and garlic. Mix well. Place around log. Take strips of peppers and form a lattice design on top of goat cheese. Place remaining peppers around cheese along with olives. Top with pine nuts and bake, covered, for 10 minutes in 350-degree oven until heated through. Serve with sprigs of rosemary or thyme on top and crostini in a basket alongside.

Serves 8 to 10

Note: Always a favorite at open houses, for a light appetizer before dinner or just as a dish to serve with wine and fruit. Can easily be made ahead, then heated just before serving.

Dilled Smoked Salmon Spread

8 ounces cream cheese, softened
1/4 cup heavy cream
1 green onion, thinly sliced
1 teaspoon fresh lemon juice
2 to 3 dashes Tabasco sauce
1/4 pound smoked salmon, shredded
1 teaspoon dried dill
fresh lemon slices
red salmon caviar (optional)
fresh dill sprigs
cocktail pumpernickel bread
English cucumber slices

In a medium bowl, mix cream cheese and heavy cream until blended. Stir in the green onion, lemon juice, Tabasco, salmon and dill. Place in a decorative 2-cup bowl or mound decoratively on a platter. Garnish with lemon slices, red caviar and dill sprigs. Refrigerate up to 24 hours before serving with pumpernickel bread triangles or sliced cucumbers.

Serves 6 to 8

Smoked Salmon Mousse

1 package gelatin
3 tablespoons cold water
3/4 cup sour cream
3/4 cup mayonnaise
4 ounces smoked salmon, finely chopped
1 tablespoon prepared horseradish

1 tablespoon chopped onion
1 tablespoon chopped fresh dill or 1 teaspoon dried dill
1 cucumber, thinly sliced
sprigs of fresh dill
1 lemon, thinly sliced

Soften gelatin in cold water in small saucepan. Heat on low and stir until dissolved. Add sour cream and mayonnaise. Stir well. Remove from heat and stir in the chopped salmon, horseradish, onion and 1 tablespoon chopped dill. Whisk well to combine. Pour into a sprayed 2-cup mold. Refrigerate until well chilled, covered with plastic wrap. (Can be made a day ahead.) Unmold onto serving platter and garnish with sliced cucumbers, fresh dill sprigs and lemon wedges. Serve with sliced baguettes or crackers.

Makes 2 cups

Crab Meat and Tomato Salsa with Toasted Pita Chips

1/2 pound crab meat (Dungeness, Blue Crab or Snow Crab)
4 large Roma tomatoes, cored and diced
1/2 cup chopped fresh cilantro
2 shallots, peeled and diced
1 jalapeño pepper, cored and diced
1/4 teaspoon salt
juice of 1 lemon or lime

1/4 cup olive oil
3 pita bread (pocket bread), each bread cut into sixths and separated (3 whole pitas, cut into sixths, then split in half, will give you 36 pieces)
1/4 cup olive oil
1/4 cup grated Romano cheese
pinch of cayenne pepper
pinch of paprika

In a mixing bowl, stir together the crab meat, diced tomatoes, cilantro, shallots, jalapeño, salt, lemon juice and oil. Refrigerate until ready to serve. Makes about 2 cups. Place pita triangles on baking sheet in a single layer. Mix together the oil, cheese, cayenne and paprika in small bowl. Brush the pita triangles with the flavored oil. Bake pita chips in a preheated 375-degree oven for 5 to 7 minutes until crispy. Serve warm with crab meat salsa.

Serves 6 to 8

Bruschetta with Tomatoes

6	Roma tomatoes, cut into 1/2-inch dice	1/4	teaspoon salt
1	clove garlic, minced	1/4	teaspoon ground black pepper
2	tablespoons extra-virgin olive oil	2	tablespoons chopped fresh basil
1	tablespoon chopped red onion	8	(1/2-inch thick) slices Italian bread
1	tablespoon red wine vinegar	2	garlic cloves, cut in half
		2	tablespoons olive oil

Have your tomato mixture made ahead before grilling bread so that the bread is still warm when topped with the tomatoes.

In a small bowl, combine the diced tomatoes, minced garlic, extra-virgin olive oil, red onion, vinegar, salt, pepper and basil. (Can be made several hours ahead. Do not refrigerate if it will be served within the hour. Tomatoes should be room temperature for full flavor.)

Rub bread on both sides with garlic halves and brush with olive oil. Toast or grill bread on both sides.

Place the 8 slices of bread on a serving platter, and top with chopped tomato mixture. Serve at once as part of an antipasto or as a perfect summer first course. Allow 2 slices of bread per person.

Serves 4

Gorgonzola and Pine Nut Canapes

4	tablespoons butter, softened	1/8	teaspoon ground black pepper
1/4	pound Gorgonzola cheese	16	slices Italian or French bread (about 3-inch diameter)
2	tablespoons chopped fresh basil		
2	tablespoons toasted pine nuts		

Place butter, Gorgonzola, basil, pine nuts and pepper in food processor. Pulse on and off until smooth, about 15 seconds. Thinly spread mixture on bread slices. (Can be made ahead up to this point.) Bake on baking sheet in 400-degree oven for 4 to 5 minutes until cheese is melted and bread is golden. Serve at once.

Makes about 16 canapes

Herb Cheese and Red Pepper Mini Tarts

1 cup (8 ounces) soft herb cheese, such as Boursin, Valfrais

1/2 red pepper, cored and cut into small dice

1 tablespoon chopped fresh basil or 1 teaspoon dried basil

1 large egg

1 sheet store-bought puff pastry, thawed and cut into $1^{1}/_{2} \times 1^{1}/_{2}$-inch squares (12 pieces)

In a small bowl, combine cheese, red pepper, basil and egg. Place a square of puff pastry in a 12-section mini muffin tin, pressing dough down into each section, leaving a bit of dough around sides. Fill each mini tart with filling, dividing evenly among the 12 tarts. Bake at 400 degrees for 12 to 15 minutes until golden and puffed. Cool for a few minutes, then remove carefully to a serving tray.

Note: Can be made ahead, frozen after allowed to cool and taken out of the tin, then reheated at 400 degrees on a baking sheet for 5 minutes.

Makes 12 tarts

Olive and Bleu Cheese Canapes

2 tablespoons olive tapenade (or olive paste)

1/4 pound bleu cheese such as Gorgonzola, Cambazola, Roquefort, softened

2 tablespoons toasted pine nuts

2 tablespoons olive oil

1 teaspoon minced garlic

12 to 15 pieces thinly sliced toasted baguette
paprika

In bowl, combine the tapenade, cheese, pine nuts, oil and garlic. Mix to a smooth consistency. Spread on sliced French bread. Place on a baking sheet and bake at 350 degrees for 5 minutes to heat through. Serve at once sprinkled lightly with paprika.

Makes about 12 to 15 pieces (4 to 6 servings)

Spiced Cheddar Rounds

1/2 cup (4-ounce stick) butter
1 cup grated very sharp Cheddar cheese
1 cup flour

1/8 teaspoon cayenne pepper
1/4 teaspoon salt
1/2 cup finely chopped fresh parsley

In food processor or mixer, cream butter until softened and then add cheese, flour, cayenne pepper and salt. Process until well combined. Remove from processor or mixer and shape into a 1 1/2-inch wide × 12-inch long log. Roll the log in the chopped fresh parsley. Wrap tightly in aluminum foil and chill at least one hour. Slice into 1/4-inch thick slices. Place slices on a parchment-lined baking sheet and bake at 400 degrees for 5 minutes. Serve at room temperature with a bowl of assorted olives and mixed nuts.

Makes about 36 slices

Note: This is such a perfect little nibble to serve as an appetizer with champagne, white or red wine and especially Martinis.

Savory Pumpkin Turnovers

2 tablespoons butter
1/4 cup finely chopped onion or shallots
    15-ounce can pumpkin purée (2 cups)
1 egg
1 teaspoon dried thyme
1/2 teaspoon salt

1/4 teaspoon white pepper
1/2 cup grated Romano cheese
1/8 teaspoon grated nutmeg
1 package (17-ounce) store-bought frozen puff pastry sheets, thawed and rolled out

In a small skillet, heat butter and sauté the onion or shallots for 3 minutes on low heat. In a small bowl, combine the pumpkin purée, sautéed onion, egg, thyme, salt, pepper, cheese and nutmeg. Place puff pastry on work surface, cut into 2×2-inch squares. Place a tablespoonful of filling in center of each pastry square. Fold over into a triangle; crimp edges with a fork. Place on parchment paper-lined baking sheet. Bake at 425 degrees for 10 to 12 minutes until puffed and golden. (Can be made ahead, baked, frozen, then reheated on a baking sheet in a 400-degree oven 5 to 8 minutes before serving.)

Makes about 24 appetizers

Stuffed Eggplant Rolls with Mozzarella, Ricotta and Tomato Sauce

2 medium eggplant, ends trimmed, cut into 1/4-inch thick slices, lengthwise (about 16 slices)
1/4 cup olive oil
8 ounces fresh mozzarella, diced into 1/2-inch cubes
2 cups (1 pound) whole milk ricotta
1/2 cup grated Romano cheese
2 eggs
1/4 cup chopped fresh parsley
1/2 teaspoon salt
1/4 teaspoon black pepper
2 cups Basic Tomato Sauce (page 84)

Garnish

1/4 cup grated Romano cheese
1/4 cup chopped fresh parsley

Place eggplant slices in a single layer on a baking sheet which has been brushed with olive oil. Brush the tops of eggplant with more olive oil. Bake in preheated 375-degree oven for 10 minutes or until the eggplant is tender. They should be able to "roll" at this point. If not, return to oven for a few more minutes. Remove from oven and cool until able to handle.

While eggplant is baking, mix mozzarella, ricotta, Romano cheese, eggs, parsley, salt and pepper in bowl until well combined. Place 1 heaping tablespoon filling in center of eggplant slice and roll up from thin end of eggplant and secure with toothpick. Repeat until all eggplant slices and filling are used. Place a thin layer of tomato sauce on bottom of 9×13-inch baking pan.

Place rolls, seam side down, in pan. Top with remaining sauce, cover loosely with foil and bake at 375 degrees for 15 minutes. Remove to serving platter and top with grated Romano cheese and chopped fresh parsley for garnish. Makes about 16 eggplant rolls. Serve 2 per person as an appetizer.

Serves 8

Curried Chicken Skewers with Apricot Glaze

2   pounds boneless, skinless chicken breasts, cut into 1-inch wide strips, removing center membrane (about 32 to 36 strips of chicken)

1   tablespoon curry powder

1/4   cup vegetable oil

2   tablespoons herbes de Provence or Italian seasoning

1   teaspoon salt

1/2   teaspoon ground black pepper

32   to 36 (6-inch) wooden skewers, soaked in water

Glaze

2   cups apricot preserves

1   tablespoon curry powder

1   cup chicken stock

1/2   cup finely chopped walnuts or pecans

1/4   cup chopped fresh parsley

Place chicken strips in bowl with curry powder, oil, herbs, salt and pepper. Marinate for 30 minutes. Thread one piece of chicken on each skewer. Bake in 375-degree oven for 5 minutes.

In a small saucepan, bring the preserves, curry powder and stock to a simmer. Brush chicken with apricot mixture and bake for an additional 5 minutes or until cooked through. Remove from oven, place on serving tray and sprinkle with finely chopped walnuts or pecans and finely chopped parsley.

Makes about 32 to 36 skewers

Miniature Crab Cakes with Chipotle Mayonnaise

1   pound crab meat
1/4   cup finely diced onion
1/4   cup finely diced red bell pepper
3   cups fresh bread crumbs (divided, 1 cup and 2 cups)
1/2   cup mayonnaise
1/4   cup cream cheese, softened

1   tablespoon Dijon mustard
1   egg
    pinch of cayenne pepper
1/8   teaspoon paprika
1/4   teaspoon salt
1   tablespoon finely chopped parsley

In a medium bowl, mix the crab meat, onion, bell pepper, 1 cup bread crumbs, mayonnaise, cream cheese, mustard, egg, cayenne, paprika, salt and parsley. Refrigerate for 1 hour. Place remaining bread crumbs in a shallow bowl. Using a tablespoon, form a crab cake about 1 inch in diameter. Coat both sides with bread crumbs and place on baking sheet which has been sprayed with vegetable or olive oil spray. Continue until all crab meat mixture is used. (Can be done a day ahead, covered with plastic wrap, then refrigerated until ready to use.) Bake at 375 degrees for 10 to 12 minutes or until golden brown. Serve warm with a small dollop of Chipotle Mayonnaise on top.

Makes about 24 mini crab cakes or 12 large crab cakes

Chipotle Mayonnaise

2   whole chipotle chilies (canned smoked jalapeño peppers)
1   cup mayonnaise

1   tablespoon minced garlic
1/2   cup chopped fresh parsley
1/4   teaspoon salt

Place all ingredients in blender or processor and blend until smooth. (Can be done a day ahead.)

Makes about 1 cup

Grilled Shrimp and Scallops with Papaya Vinaigrette on Mixed Greens

8   large scallops
8   large raw shrimp, peeled and deveined
4   (6-inch) wooden skewers soaked in water 10 minutes
2   tablespoons olive oil mixed with 1 clove minced garlic, 1 teaspoon salt and 1/4 teaspoon black pepper
4   cups mixed greens
1   papaya, peeled and diced

juice of 1 lime
2   tablespoons rice wine vinegar
2   tablespoons vegetable oil
2   tablespoons sugar
2   tablespoons chopped fresh mint
1   teaspoon salt
1/8 teaspoon ground white pepper
4   lime slices
4   mint sprigs

Skewer 2 shrimp and 2 scallops per skewer. Place on grill. Brush with olive oil mixture. Cook on all sides until shrimp are pink and scallops are opaque. Remove to platter. Place 1 cup greens on each of 4 serving plates. Combine the diced papaya, lime juice, vinegar, oil, sugar, mint, salt and pepper in mixing bowl. Whisk. Place one skewer of seafood on each platter. Top each with 1/4 of papaya vinaigrette. Garnish with fresh lime slice and a fresh mint sprig. Serve at once.

Serves 4

Lemon Garlic Shrimp

2   pounds peeled, deveined and cooked large shrimp (21 to 26 per pound), tails on
1/4 cup olive oil
2   lemons, zest and juice
1/4 cup chopped fresh parsley

1   tablespoon minced garlic
1   tablespoon chopped fresh dill or 1 teaspoon dried dill
1/2 teaspoon salt
    pinch of red pepper flakes

In a bowl, combine all ingredients. Stir well. Taste for seasoning. Cover; refrigerate until ready to use. Serve with lemon slices and parsley sprigs. (Can be made hours ahead.)

Serves 8 to 10, allowing 5 to 6 shrimp per person

Note: This is a popular appetizer that we have made at Cucina for years. It is easy, can be made ahead and is always a hit with guests.

Pissaladière (Onion and Olive Tart)

1	sheet store-bought puff pastry, thawed and rolled out	2	large onions, thinly sliced
4	tablespoons olive tapenade (or olive paste)	1	teaspoon dried thyme
			4-ounce log goat cheese
4	tablespoons butter	1/4	cup chopped fresh parsley

Place puff pastry on parchment paper on baking sheet. Crimp edges. Spread tapenade on pastry. In medium skillet, heat butter and sauté onion until golden brown on medium heat (onion should be caramelized) for about 10 minutes. Remove from heat and stir in the thyme. Spread onions over olive tapenade, dot with goat cheese and bake in preheated 450-degree oven for 15 minutes or until pastry is puffed and golden. Remove from oven, top with chopped parsley and cut into bite-sized pieces.

Serves 8 to 10

Roma Tomato, Goat Cheese and Basil Tart

2	sheets store-bought puff pastry, placed side by side on a baking sheet lined with parchment paper	8	ounces goat cheese
		1	cup fresh basil leaves, coarsely chopped
4	ounces (1/2 cup) pesto—your choice of olive, basil, sun-dried tomato	1	cup shredded Parmesan cheese
		2	tablespoons olive oil
8	large Roma tomatoes, each cut into 5 slices (don't use ends)	1	teaspoon kosher salt
		1/2	teaspoon ground black pepper

Seal the two pieces of pastry in the center. Crimp the edges slightly. Brush the pastry lightly with pesto of choice. Place the sliced tomatoes in neat rows down and across. You should have 8 slices × 5 slices (40 tomato slices). Dollop the goat cheese over the tomatoes. Sprinkle basil and shredded Parmesan cheese on top, drizzle with olive oil, kosher salt and pepper. Bake in 400-degree oven for 15 minutes or until pastry is golden and cheese is melted. Cool slightly. Using a pizza cutter, cut squares around each tomato.

Makes 40 pieces

Antipasto Platter with Pizzazz

*Antipasto platters (before pasta, translation) are as diversified as the cook.
Remember color, texture and taste . . . make it your special creation. Some of the
items (there should be at least 4 to 5) on a tray could be:*

olives—3 or 4 varieties
roasted pepper strips
dolmathes (stuffed grape leaves)
sliced mozzarella and tomatoes with basil
sliced salami, soppressata or pepperoni
mortadella cubes
provolone cubes
crostini with white bean dip
baby mozzarella balls with oil and basil
sliced prosciutto or prosciutto "roses"
chunks of Reggiano, Parmesan or Asiago
    cheese drizzled with good quality
    balsamic vinegar

tuna and bean salad
shrimp and bean salad
caponata (Sicilian eggplant relish)
grilled vegetables
marinated mushrooms and/or artichokes
marinated artichoke hearts mixed with
    red peppers
garbanzo beans with a black olive
    tapenade

Many of these items can be purchased at your local Italian deli or in the specialty section of
your supermarket. Remember crusty bread slices and garnishes such as rosemary or basil. Many
antipasto dishes can be served in place of meals when there are enough varieties on the platter.
Have fun, be creative and there are really no rules, except use the best ingredients you can find!

Breakfast, Brunch and Breads

Savor the Memories of Sunday mornings in New York...
of hot semolina breads from the Italian bakery;
fresh bagels with cream cheese, red onions, capers, and lox;
and The New York Times.

Smoked Salmon Frittata

8	large eggs	4	ounces cream cheese, cubed
1 1/2	cups half-and-half	1/4	cup chopped fresh chives or green onions
1/2	teaspoon salt		
1/4	teaspoon black pepper	2	tablespoons butter
1/4	pound smoked salmon, cut into 1-inch pieces	1	tablespoon olive oil

Garnish

2 tablespoons chopped fresh chives or green onions

In medium bowl, beat eggs with half-and-half and salt and pepper until eggs are frothy. Stir in the smoked salmon, cream cheese and chives. Heat butter and olive oil in 10-inch nonstick ovenproof skillet over medium heat. When butter is hot, add the egg mixture, and cook on medium heat for 3 minutes. Do not stir.

Place skillet on center rack of a preheated 400-degree oven. Bake for 15 minutes or until frittata is puffed and center is cooked through. Loosen the edges of the frittata and invert onto a large platter, then invert again so the top is facing up. Sprinkle with more chopped chives, if desired. Cut into 6 wedges. Serve at once.

Serves 6

Red Pepper and Sausage Frittata

1	tablespoon olive oil		10	large eggs
1	tablespoon butter		1	cup half-and-half
1	small red pepper, cored and diced		1/2	teaspoon salt
2	tablespoons chopped onion		1/4	teaspoon ground black pepper
1	teaspoon chopped garlic		1/2	cup shredded mozzarella
1/2	pound bulk Italian sausage		1/4	cup chopped fresh basil

In a 10-inch ovenproof nonstick skillet, heat the oil and butter. Add red pepper and onion and sauté until onion is soft, about 3 minutes. Add the garlic and sausage. Sauté for 5 minutes, crumbling sausage as it cooks; drain sausage of excess fat.

In a medium bowl, beat the eggs, half-and-half, salt and pepper until frothy. Pour eggs over the sausage and pepper. Cook on medium heat for 3 minutes, allowing eggs to cook slightly around the edges. Top eggs with mozzarella and bake the frittata in a preheated 400-degree oven for 12 to 15 minutes or until eggs are set and puffed. Remove from oven, top with chopped basil, slide the frittata onto a serving plate and cut into 6 wedges.

Serves 6

Frittatas are so easy to prepare and with the help of a nonstick skillet, it is easier to serve without worry of eggs sticking to the pan. You can alter the ingredients to your taste; just remember to cook the frittata on top of the stove first, then finish it off in the oven. It is a great way to serve a group of hungry people in a hurry. We have been serving frittatas of one flavor or another for breakfast at Cucina since we opened. They are always a hit!

Grandma Mary's Spinach and Sausage Pie

1 recipe Classic Pizza Dough (page 110)
4 tablespoons olive oil
1 tablespoon minced garlic
  pinch red pepper flakes
1/2 pound sweet bulk Italian sausage

1 1/2 pounds to 2 pounds fresh spinach leaves, cleaned
1/8 teaspoon nutmeg
1/2 teaspoon salt
1/2 cup grated Romano cheese
2 tablespoons olive oil

Divide the pizza dough into 2 pieces. Roll each piece out to 10-inch diameter circles. Place one piece of dough in a 9-inch pie plate, leaving the dough overlapping the side of the pan. Set aside.

Heat the olive oil in large skillet. Add garlic and red pepper flakes. Sauté for 1 minute on low heat. Add sausage and cook until no longer pink, crumbling sausage as you cook. Add the spinach leaves, nutmeg and salt. Cover skillet, cook on medium for 3 to 4 minutes, stirring often, just until spinach leaves are slightly wilted but not cooked through. Drain off the excess water in pan and add spinach and sausage mixture to the pizza dough-lined pie plate. Sprinkle on the Romano cheese.

Top with second piece of dough, crimping and securing the edges of the dough. Brush the top of the dough with the 2 tablespoons olive oil. Cut three or four 1-inch slits in the dough for steam to escape. Bake in a preheated 400-degree oven for 20 to 25 minutes or until the dough is golden and crispy. Remove the pie from oven, and allow to cool for 10 minutes before slicing into 8 wedges.

Serves 8

My grandmother, Mary Filippi was 4 feet 9 inches. She was a pistol. Don't ever cross Grandma. Her Sicilian blood ran thick and deep. She never learned to speak English properly, instead spoke with a thick Italian accent. She came from a wealthy family of olive farmers back in Alcamo, Sicily, and could never quite get over the fact that her husband brought her to America where she had to work hard for everything she had.
She was a great pizza and pasta maker but not a very good everyday cook.
We all knew when Grandma, or Nanny, as the grandkids called her, was making pizza. The house would be filled with the aroma of tomato sauce, the yeasty dough would be rising in the oven and the large baking pans greased and ready to be filled with the risen dough, sauce and myriad of toppings such as cheese, anchovies, olives and prosciutto. I remember coming home from school, opening the front door and seeing Grandma, about as tall as the kitchen table, rolling out the dough to make her spinach pie. It was grand. Of course the sausage would be left out of the pie if it were a Friday, since we couldn't have meat. Oh, but it was great, even though.

Torta Rustica (Rustic Italian Pie)

Crust

2   to 2$^1/_2$ cups flour
4   ounces (1 stick) butter, cut into 8 pieces

2   large eggs
$^1/_8$ teaspoon salt
     about $^1/_4$ cup iced water

Place flour, butter, eggs and salt in food processor. Pulse on and off for 10 seconds. Slowly add the iced water until dough forms a soft ball. Do not overprocess. Remove to a floured work surface and form into a large ball. Divide the dough into 2 pieces, one about $^2/_3$ of the dough, the other $^1/_3$ of the dough. Roll out the larger piece to a 12-inch diameter and place in a 9-inch springform pan so it comes up the sides and overlaps the pan slightly. Roll out the smaller piece of dough to a 9-inch diameter and cut into twelve $^1/_2$-inch wide strips. This will form the "lattice" on top of pie. Set aside.

Filling

2   pounds whole milk ricotta
1   pound fresh mozzarella, cubed or shredded
4   large eggs
$^1/_2$ cup grated Romano or Parmesan cheese
$^1/_4$ pound sliced Genoa salami, cut into thin strips

$^1/_4$ pound ham or cappacolla (spicy ham), cut into thin strips
$^1/_4$ pound sliced prosciutto, cut into thin strips
$^1/_8$ teaspoon nutmeg
$^1/_4$ teaspoon salt
$^1/_2$ teaspoon ground black pepper

Egg Wash

1   egg beaten with 1 tablespoon cream

In a mixing bowl, stir all ingredients for filling together until well combined. Pour into pastry-lined springform pan. Smooth to level the cheese filling. Loosely place 6 strips of dough in one direction on top of pie. Place 6 strips in opposite direction to form a "lattice" on top of pie. Crimp edges of lattice with the bottom layer of pie crust. Brush top of pie with egg wash. Bake in a 350-degree oven for 1 hour until golden brown and center is set. Remove from oven. Allow to cool to room temperature before slicing. (If pie is too hot, the cheese will run out and not remain in solid form when cutting.) Remove outer ring of springform pan and cut into 8 wedges.

Serves 8

Note: There is no Easter without this traditional pie served on Easter morning or as part of Easter dinner. Can be made a day ahead, then reheated in the springform pan for 10 minutes in a 400-degree oven to get the chill out.

Jones Beach Peppers and Eggs

4	tablespoons olive oil	1/4	cup water
1	large onion, thinly sliced	1	teaspoon salt
2	green bell peppers, cored and thinly sliced	1/4	teaspoon ground black pepper
12	large eggs	1	loaf Italian bread about 4 inches wide, 12 inches long

In a large skillet, heat olive oil. Sauté the onion and peppers for 5 minutes on medium heat, stirring often. In a medium bowl, beat the eggs, water, salt and pepper until frothy. Add to skillet with onion and peppers. Stir eggs until eggs are scrambled and are cooked through.

Slice the bread horizontally, scoop out some of the soft bread on bottom half of the bread to make a "bed" for the eggs and place peppers and eggs in the loaf of bread. Place top of bread on eggs to make a large sandwich, wrap in foil and take along on your next picnic or beach outing. Cut sandwich into 2-inch wide pieces.

Serves 6

This was a staple take along back in the 60s, when my family would head to Jones Beach, Long Island, bright and early on Saturdays or Sundays in the summer months, fighting traffic along the way. When we would finally set down our blankets and umbrellas, the pepper and egg sandwiches, along with orange juice and coffee would be served immediately. They were terrific. It kept us going until lunch, when it would be fruits, cheeses and Italian cold cuts. Then in the evening, after swimming and sunning all day, the family would carry our red Coca-Cola logo cooler to the picnic area where we would grill steaks, slice tomatoes from the garden and have more food that seemed never to run out. The cousins, aunts and uncles would all participate in the preparation of the meals, and food would magically appear from the cooler. When we finally would head home in the dark, again in traffic, we were tired, sunburned but totally satiated. The first time I brought my husband to this ritual in 1969, he couldn't believe the feast on the beach!

Shrimp, Spinach and Feta Egg Puff

2	tablespoons butter		1/4	pound feta cheese, crumbled
1/4	cup chopped onion		1	teaspoon dried oregano
10	ounces fresh spinach leaves, washed		10	large eggs
1/8	teaspoon nutmeg		2	cups half-and-half
1	teaspoon salt		1/2	cup flour
1/4	teaspoon ground black pepper			
1	pound large shrimp, cooked and tails removed			

In a large skillet, heat the butter and sauté onion until soft. Add spinach, nutmeg, salt and pepper. Cover; simmer until spinach is wilted. Add the shrimp, cheese and oregano and toss well. Set aside.

In a large bowl, beat the eggs with half-and-half and flour until flour is well incorporated. There should be no bits of flour in the mixture. Add the spinach, shrimp, and feta mixture, draining off excess water first. Mix well. Pour the egg mixture into a greased 12-inch diameter baking dish, such as a ceramic quiche pan.

Bake in a preheated 375-degree oven for 25 minutes or until puffed and golden. Cut into 6 to 8 wedges. Serve at once.

Serves 6 to 8

Note: I love making egg puffs for breakfast or brunch for a crowd. The addition of the flour to the eggs gives the puff more body, allows it to be firm, yet still puffy. You can use the egg and half-and-half as a base and add or delete any ingredients you'd like.

Orange French Toast

4   large eggs
1   cup half-and-half
     zest and juice of 1 large orange
2   tablespoons brown sugar
1   teaspoon vanilla extract
1   teaspoon cinnamon

8   to 10 thick (1-inch) slices Italian or
     French bread
2   tablespoons butter
     powdered sugar
     warmed maple syrup or Orange
     Maple Syrup

In a medium bowl, whisk together the eggs, half-and-half, orange zest and juice, brown sugar, vanilla extract and cinnamon. Dip the bread in egg mixture and cook in the butter in a large skillet for 3 to 4 minutes per side. Serve with powdered sugar and warmed maple syrup or Orange Maple Syrup.

Serves 4 to 5; 2 slices per person

Orange Maple Syrup

2   tablespoons water
3/4   cup brown sugar
1/2   cup orange juice concentrate
4   ounces (1 stick) butter

1/4   cup pure maple syrup
     zest of 1 orange
1/2   cup honey

In a medium saucepan, bring water, brown sugar and orange juice to a simmer. Add the butter, maple syrup, orange zest and honey. Cook on low heat for 5 minutes. Serve warm over pancakes, French toast or waffles. Refrigerate any leftover syrup and then reheat as needed.

Makes about 1 1/2 cups syrup

Blueberry Corn Bread

3/4	cup sugar		3/4	teaspoon salt
2	large eggs		1 1/2	cups whole milk
2	cups flour		1	tablespoon melted butter
1	cup yellow cornmeal		1	cup fresh blueberries or 1 cup frozen
1	tablespoon baking powder			blueberries, thawed

In a mixing bowl, beat sugar and eggs together until fluffy and lemon-colored. Stir in the flour, cornmeal, baking powder, salt, milk and melted butter. Fold in the blueberries. Pour batter into an 8×8-inch greased and floured baking pan. Bake in a preheated 425-degree oven for 30 minutes or until corn bread is set in center. Let cool in pan for 10 minutes, then cut into 9 servings.

Serves 9

Orange Date Nut Bread

1	medium orange		1	beaten large egg
2	cups flour		1/2	cup water
1/2	cup sugar		3	tablespoons melted butter
2	teaspoons baking powder		1	cup pitted and chopped dates
1/2	teaspoon baking soda		3/4	cup chopped walnuts
1/2	teaspoon salt			

Quarter the orange, remove the seeds and place the quartered orange in a food processor or blender. Purée. Set aside. In a mixing bowl, combine the flour, sugar, baking powder, baking soda and salt. Add the egg, water, melted butter and puréed orange to dry ingredients. Fold in the dates and nuts. Pour the batter into a greased and floured 9×5×3-inch loaf pan. Bake in a 350-degree oven for 60 to 70 minutes until center is set. Cool the bread in the pan for 10 minutes, turn out onto wire rack and allow to cool to room temperature before slicing.

Makes 1 loaf

Note: This bread freezes well.

Best-Ever Pumpkin Nut Bread

1 1/2 cups pumpkin purée
1 cup sugar
1/3 cup whole milk
1/4 cup vegetable or canola oil
2 cups flour
2 teaspoons baking soda

1 teaspoon cinnamon
1/2 teaspoon ground cloves
1/2 teaspoon ground ginger
1/2 teaspoon salt
1 teaspoon orange zest
1/2 cup chopped pecans or walnuts

In a mixer bowl, beat the pumpkin purée and sugar for 1 minute on medium speed. Beat in the milk, oil, flour, baking soda, cinnamon, cloves, ginger, salt and orange zest until well combined. Do not overbeat. Stir in the nuts. Pour batter into a greased and floured 9×5×3-inch loaf pan. Bake in preheated 350-degree oven for 55 minutes to 1 hour. Cool bread in pan for 10 minutes, then turn out onto cake rack. Cool to room temperature before slicing.

Makes 1 loaf

Strawberry Nut Bread

4 large eggs
2 (10-ounce) packages frozen strawberries, thawed
1 cup vegetable or canola oil
1 cup sugar
3 cups flour
1 teaspoon cinnamon

1 teaspoon nutmeg
1 teaspoon baking soda
1 teaspoon salt
1 1/4 cups chopped nuts of choice: walnut, pecan, almond, macadamia, hazelnut

In a mixer bowl, beat eggs until frothy. Beat in the thawed strawberries, oil, sugar, flour, cinnamon, nutmeg, baking soda and salt. Beat on medium speed for 1 minute until well blended, but not overmixed. Stir in nuts. Pour batter into 2 greased and floured 9×5×3-inch loaf pans. Bake in preheated 350-degree oven for 1 hour and 10 minutes. Cool bread in pans for 10 minutes, then turn out onto cake racks.

Makes 2 loaves

Note: Substitute the strawberries with raspberries for a change of flavor. Serve this bread with softened cream cheese, a rich unsalted butter or just as is . . . a perfect brunch bread. This bread freezes well and it is best sliced when cooled.

Quick Irish Soda Bread

2	cups flour		$1/2$	stick (2 ounces) butter
$1/2$	teaspoon baking soda		$1/2$	cup raisins or currants
$1^1/2$	teaspoons baking powder		1	teaspoon caraway seeds (optional)
$1/2$	teaspoon salt		$1/2$	to $2/3$ cup buttermilk
1	tablespoon sugar		2	tablespoons whole milk

Sift the flour, baking soda, baking powder, salt and sugar together in a large mixing bowl. With a pastry blender (or in the food processor), cut in the butter until mixture is the size of peas. Stir in the raisins or currants (and caraway seeds, if you choose to add them), and gradually add the buttermilk until mixture is moist. Knead on a floured board for 1 minute.

Shape the dough into a round loaf, place on a greased and floured baking pan. Cut an "X" on the top, brush with the whole milk and bake in a preheated 375-degree oven for 40 to 45 minutes. Tap for doneness . . . if the bread sounds hollow on top, it is done. Allow to cool to room temperature before cutting.

Makes one 8-inch round loaf

Fugazza di Pasqua (Italian Easter Bread)

3	to 3¹/₄ cups bread flour	2	large eggs
¹/₄	cup sugar	1	teaspoon lemon extract and zest of
1	teaspoon salt		1 lemon or 1 teaspoon anise extract
1	package active dry yeast (or	5	hard-boiled colored eggs
	1 heaping tablespoon bottled yeast)	¹/₂	cup powdered sugar mixed with
²/₃	cup whole milk		1 tablespoon milk or cream for glaze
2	tablespoons butter		colored sprinkle candies

In mixing bowl of electric mixer, combine 1 cup flour, sugar, salt and yeast. In a small saucepan, heat milk and butter until lukewarm. Add to dry ingredients and beat for 2 minutes on medium speed. Add the eggs and 1 cup flour. Add extract of choice and another cup of flour. With dough hook, knead dough for 5 minutes in mixer. Remove dough and place in greased bowl and turn once to grease the top of dough. Cover; place in draft-free place and allow the dough to double in size, about 1 hour.

Punch the dough down. Divide dough in half. Roll each half into a 24-inch long rope on a floured board. On a greased baking pan, place the two ropes in a circular twist to form a ring. Place the hard-boiled colored eggs tucked into dough, 1 in the center and 4 on the perimeter. Cover loosely with plastic wrap or a dishtowel; allow the dough to rise 30 minutes. Bake in 350-degree oven for 30 to 35 minutes until golden brown. Remove from oven and while warm, brush top with powdered sugar glaze and sprinkle with colored candies.

Makes one 12-inch diameter bread

I have been making these traditional Easter breads every year for the past 30 years. They have become legendary among friends and family and Good Friday would not be the same without the aroma of lemon and anise wafting through the kitchen. I usually make about 10 large breads, using lemon in half the recipes and anise in the other half. They are beautiful when baked and sprinkled with colored candies and make a spectacular presentation as an Easter gift to your neighbors, wrapped in colored cellophane and tied with a big purple bow.

Salads

*Savor the Memories of hot, humid days in Brooklyn,
and my grandmother tending her prolific tomato plants...
our summer garden-fresh tomatoes, thickly sliced and
topped with hearty leaves of fresh basil, fragrant
olive oil, coarse salt, and freshly ground black pepper.*

Greek Cucumber Tomato Salad

4   large red tomatoes, each cored and cut into 12 wedges

2   large cucumbers, peeled, cut in half lengthwise, seeded and sliced

1   small red onion, peeled, thinly sliced

1/2   cup pitted kalamata olives

1   cup crumbled feta cheese

1/2   cup chopped fresh parsley

1/4   cup olive oil

3   tablespoons red wine vinegar

1   teaspoon salt

1/4   teaspoon ground black pepper

Combine the tomatoes, cucumber slices, red onion, olives, feta and parsley in a medium bowl. Toss in the olive oil, red wine vinegar, salt and pepper. Serve at once.

Serves 6 to 8

Note: Cucina's Cucumber Tomato Salad or Greek salad is so popular, we have had to double the original recipe over the years. It is a favorite of people on low-fat diets, people who love the cool, crisp flavors and children love the feta and olives.

Spicy Corn and Bean Fiesta

16-ounce bag frozen corn kernels, thawed at room temperature

15-ounce can black beans, drained and rinsed

1   small red pepper, cored and diced

1   small green pepper, cored and diced

1   small red onion, diced

1   bunch fresh cilantro, chopped

1   jalapeño pepper, cored and diced juice of 1 lime

2   teaspoons chili powder

2   teaspoons cumin powder

1   tablespoon sugar

1/4   cup white or cider vinegar

1/2   cup vegetable or canola oil

1   teaspoon salt

Combine all ingredients in a bowl. Toss well. Taste for seasoning. Chill 1 hour before serving.

Serves 8 to 10

Note: This has been a favorite of Cucina's customers from the first day we served it in 1995. It is one of our most requested recipes and will be one of yours, too. We love it served next to grilled chicken, pork roast or a grilled thick tenderloin steak.

Cucina's Festive Mixed Greens

Salad

1	cup pecan halves	1	red onion, thinly sliced
1/4	cup sugar	2	navel or blood oranges, peeled and thinly sliced
8	cups mixed greens		
1/2	cup sun-dried cranberries	2	pears, cored and thinly sliced
1	cup crumbled bleu cheese, such as Gorgonzola		

Place pecan halves and sugar in a small sauté pan over low heat. Cook for 2 to 3 minutes, shaking often, just until sugar starts to dissolve and pecans are coated with the sugar. Remove from heat, cool to room temperature and break up the pecan halves if they have stuck together.

Place the greens evenly on a large serving platter. Sprinkle with cranberries, bleu cheese and sliced onion. Place the oranges around the perimeter of platter with pear slices in between the orange slices. Sprinkle on the sugared pecans.

Dressing

4	tablespoons pear, raspberry or other fruit-flavored vinegar	1/2	teaspoon salt
		1/4	teaspoon ground black pepper
1	tablespoon Dijon mustard	1/2	cup vegetable or canola oil

For dressing, combine the vinegar, mustard, salt and pepper in a small bowl. Whisk in the oil, until incorporated. Pour evenly over salad and serve at once.

Serves 6 to 8

Note: This is such a colorful salad that we created at Cucina, it has become a signature salad for us, especially in the fall, when we add pomegranate seeds on top of the salad for a jeweled effect.

Marguerite's Caprese Salad

2   cups fresh mixed greens
2   large ripe red tomatoes, ends trimmed, each cut into 4 thick slices
1   pound fresh mozzarella, cut into 16 slices
16 leaves fresh basil
2   yellow tomatoes, ends trimmed, each cut into 4 thick slices

1   red onion, thinly sliced
2   tablespoons capers
1/4 cup extra-virgin olive oil
1   teaspoon kosher salt
1/2 teaspoon coarsely ground pepper

Place mixed greens on serving platter. Alternate a tomato slice, mozzarella slice, basil leaf, yellow tomato slice, mozzarella slice, basil leaf, etc., in a concentric circle on the mixed greens. Separate the red onion rings and place over the tomatoes, sprinkle on the capers, drizzle on the olive oil, sprinkle on salt and pepper.

Serves 4 to 6

Note: There are many versions of Caprese salad, but I like this salad with the addition of the capers and onions. I don't use vinegar on this salad because it changes the fresh flavor of the mozzarella . . . use your best extra-virgin olive oil for this salad. I like the red and yellow tomatoes for contrast, but when yellow tomatoes are not in season, use the best red tomatoes you can find. I also look for heirloom tomatoes in the farmers' markets in summer. They add a different dimension to the salad, too.

Mixed Greens with Warmed Basil, Tomato and Goat Cheese Salad

4	to 6 cups mixed greens	4	ounces goat cheese
2	tablespoons olive oil	1/4	cup olive oil
1	tablespoon chopped garlic		juice of 1 lemon
1	pint cherry tomatoes or pear-shaped tomatoes	1/2	teaspoon salt
1/4	cup chopped fresh basil	1/4	teaspoon ground black pepper

Place greens in salad bowl. In small saucepan, heat oil. Add garlic and tomatoes and sauté for 2 minutes on medium heat until tomatoes are heated through. Remove from heat, add basil and goat cheese. Toss into greens, then toss with olive oil, lemon juice, salt and pepper. Serve at once.

Serves 4 to 6

Cumin-Scented Mushroom Salad

1	pound button mushrooms, cleaned	2	tablespoons chopped fresh parsley
1	red bell pepper, cored and cut into julienne strips	1/4	to 1/2 teaspoon ground cumin or cumin seeds
1/4	cup fruity olive oil	1	teaspoon salt
	juice of 1 lemon	1/2	teaspoon ground black pepper
1	tablespoon minced garlic		

Leave the mushrooms whole if they are small; otherwise, cut into halves or quarters. Combine the red peppers, mushrooms, olive oil, lemon juice, garlic, parsley, cumin and salt and pepper in bowl. Toss gently. Refrigerate up to 6 hours before serving.

Serves 4 to 6

Panzanella (Tuscan Bread Salad)

This is a classic summertime salad, using fresh tomatoes and basil from the garden . . . it can be made ahead and is the perfect accompaniment to any grilled meat or fish entrée.

1 pound loaf Filone or other hearty Italian bread	1/4 cup extra-virgin olive oil
1/4 cup extra-virgin olive oil	3 tablespoons red wine vinegar
2 cloves garlic, minced	1/2 teaspoon salt
8 large ripe beefsteak tomatoes	1/4 teaspoon ground black pepper
1/4 cup sliced red onion	1/2 cup shaved Romano pecorino cheese
1 bunch (about 1 cup) fresh basil leaves, coarsely chopped	

Cut bread into 1-inch cubes. In bowl, toss bread with the 1/4 cup olive oil and 2 cloves minced garlic. Place on baking sheet and bake for 10 minutes in 350-degree oven. Bread should be crisp and golden on outside.

Cut tomatoes into 1-inch pieces; place in bowl with red onion, basil leaves, the 1/4 cup olive oil, vinegar, salt and pepper. Toss in toasted bread. Allow to sit for 1/2 hour, tossing often. Bread should be soft and saturated slightly with the oil and vinegar. Taste for seasoning. Serve with shaved Romano cheese on top.

Serves 8

Note: You can add 1 pound grilled shrimp, 1/2 cup kalamata olives or 4 grilled chicken breast halves (1 pound) cut into strips for a complete one-dish meal.

Penne alla Siciliana

A great pasta salad from Cucina

1	pound imported penne pasta	2	pounds Roma tomatoes, cored and coarsely chopped
1	tablespoon minced garlic		
1/4	cup fresh basil leaves	1/2	teaspoon salt
1/4	cup fresh oregano leaves	1/4	teaspoon ground black pepper
1/4	cup fresh parsley	1/2	cup extra-virgin olive oil
1/4	cup fresh mint leaves	1/2	cup shredded Parmesan cheese

Cook pasta al dente, then rinse under cold water to stop cooking process. Drain and set aside in a large bowl.

In a food processor, place the garlic, herbs, tomatoes, salt and pepper. Pulse on and off 5 times. You want the mixture to look like a salsa, not puréed. The tomatoes should have some texture and the herbs should be chopped. Add the oil and pulse on and off once. Pour the sauce over the pasta and toss well. Taste for seasoning. Toss in the shredded cheese.

Serves 8

Note: This sauce is wonderful at the peak of summer's bounty, but we make it all year round. The fresh, simple flavors of the fresh herbs and garlic, tomatoes and olive oil and just a hint of cheese blend beautifully for this pasta salad. I know it will be one of your favorites, too.

Mediterranean Potato Salad

3	pounds new potatoes	1	tablespoon minced garlic
1	tablespoon salt	$1/2$	cup olive oil
2	medium tomatoes, diced	$1/4$	cup red wine vinegar
$1/2$	cup chopped red onion	1	teaspoon salt
$1/2$	cup pitted kalamata olives, sliced in half	$1/2$	teaspoon ground black pepper
1	tablespoon capers	2	tablespoons chopped fresh parsley

Cut potatoes into 1-inch cubes. Bring water seasoned with the 1 tablespoon salt to a boil, add the potatoes and cook on medium heat until tender, about 15 minutes. Don't have the water at a full boil, but rather a simmer. This keeps the potatoes from breaking down. Drain and cool the potatoes to room temperature.

In medium bowl, combine the tomatoes, onion, olives, capers and garlic. Add potatoes and toss. In small bowl, whisk the oil, vinegar, salt, pepper and parsley. Gently toss dressing into salad. Refrigerate at least 1 hour before serving.

Serves 6 to 8

Note: This is the perfect take-along potato salad for picnics . . . no mayonnaise to worry about. It even tastes better made earlier in the day. I prefer the red or white new potatoes for this recipe. They have a better consistency and will not fall apart in the salad.

Italian Beef Salad on Greens

3	to 3¹/2 pounds beef tenderloin, sirloin, tri-tip or other lean cut of boneless beef		6	cups mixed spring greens
2	tablespoons kosher salt		1	head radicchio, cored and cut into thin strips
1	tablespoon coarsely ground pepper		6	navel oranges, peeled and thinly sliced
1	tablespoon herbes de Provence or 1 teaspoon each: dried thyme, dried oregano and dried parsley		2	red onions, peeled and thinly sliced

Rub the beef with the kosher salt, pepper and herbs. Set oven to 500 degrees. Place beef on roasting pan and roast for 15 minutes; reduce heat to 325 degrees and roast until beef is medium rare, about 15 minutes per pound. Test with meat thermometer; it should read 145 degrees. Allow beef to "rest" 5 minutes before slicing. (This can be done earlier in day and then refrigerated until ready to use.) Slice thinly against grain of beef.

Place the greens and radicchio on a decorative serving platter. Place thinly sliced beef on greens in a concentric circle in center of platter. Place the orange slices and onions around perimeter of platter.

Dressing

³/4	cup olive oil		1	tablespoon Dijon mustard
¹/4	cup red wine vinegar		1	tablespoon horseradish
1	tablespoon chopped fresh garlic		1	teaspoon salt
1	tablespoon capers		¹/2	teaspoon black pepper

Garnish

¹/2	cup toasted and chopped pecans, walnuts or almonds	fresh sprigs of herbs such as thyme, basil or parsley

Make dressing by whisking all ingredients in a small bowl. Drizzle on top of beef, oranges and onions just before ready to serve. Serve at once with chopped nuts, sprigs of herbs and freshly ground pepper on top.

Serves 6 to 8

Note: This is such an easy, impressive dish for summer lunches, buffet dinner or just a casual dinner on the patio. The orange and purple colors are vibrant against the greens, and the textures and flavors meld beautifully.

Cucina's Curried Chicken Salad

2   pounds boneless, skinless cold
    poached chicken breasts, cut into
    1-inch dice
4   ribs celery, thinly sliced on diagonal

2   cups red grapes
1/2 cup chopped walnuts
1/2 cup golden raisins

In a large mixing bowl, combine the poached chicken, sliced celery, red grapes, walnuts and raisins.

Dressing

1   cup mayonnaise
1/4 cup half-and-half
1/2 cup apricot preserves
1/4 cup rice wine vinegar

2   tablespoons curry powder
1/2 teaspoon salt
1/2 teaspoon white pepper

In a small bowl, whisk together all ingredients for dressing. Gently fold the dressing into the salad. Refrigerate for at least 1 hour before serving.

Serves 8

Note: Since we started serving this salad, not a day goes by when we don't sell out. It is easy, flavorful and with the addition of the apricot preserves, it gives the salad a sweet tangy edge to the chicken. The perfect luncheon salad, over greens, or just in a thick roll for a great sandwich.

Pesto Farfalle and Chicken Salad

Basil Pesto

1   cup fresh basil leaves
1   cup fresh spinach leaves
2   tablespoons minced garlic
1/4   cup pine nuts
1/4   cup grated Romano cheese

1/2   teaspoon salt
1/4   teaspoon ground black pepper
1/2   cup olive oil
1/2   cup vegetable oil

In a food processor, place the basil leaves, spinach leaves, garlic, pine nuts, cheese, salt and pepper. Pulse on and off 5 to 6 times to chop the basil and spinach. With the motor running, add the olive and vegetable oils in a slow stream. Pesto should be creamy in texture. Taste for seasoning.

Makes about 2 cups pesto

Salad

1   pound imported farfalle (bowtie) pasta
2   tablespoons olive oil
1   large onion, thinly sliced (use a sweet onion, such as Vidalia, Walla Walla or Maui, if available)

2   pounds boneless, skinless chicken breasts, grilled or broiled
1   cup sun-dried cranberries

Cook pasta until "al dente," then drain and rinse under cold water to stop cooking process. Set aside in a large mixing bowl.

Heat the olive oil in a medium skillet. Sauté the onion until golden, about 7 to 10 minutes. Add to pasta. Cut the cooked chicken breasts into 1-inch pieces and add to pasta along with the sun-dried cranberries. Gently stir the basil pesto into pasta mixture until it is coated with the pesto. Taste for seasoning and add more salt and pepper at this point, if needed.

Serves 6 to 8

Mosaic Chicken Salad

1	head red leaf lettuce, washed and dried	1	pound fresh asparagus spears, trimmed and cut into 1-inch pieces
2	whole boneless, skinless chicken breasts (about 2 pounds)	1	red bell pepper, cored and cut into thin strips
1/2	to 1 cup chicken broth, white wine or water	1	yellow bell pepper, cored and cut into thin strips
	10-ounce package frozen artichoke hearts, thawed, or 15-ounce can artichoke hearts, drained	1/2	cup feta cheese, crumbled
		1	small red onion, thinly sliced

Line serving platter with red leaf lettuce.

Poach chicken breasts in broth, wine or water until cooked through. Cool. Cut into 1/2×1-inch thick strips.

In a medium skillet, cook the frozen artichoke hearts (if using them) and asparagus in 2 inches of water until tender, about 2 minutes. Drain and cool to room temperature.

In mixing bowl, combine the chicken, artichokes, asparagus, red and yellow peppers, feta cheese and red onion. Toss gently. Place on lettuce leaves.

Dressing

	juice and zest of 1 lemon	1/2	teaspoon salt
1/4	cup chopped fresh basil	1/4	teaspoon ground black pepper
2	tablespoons red wine vinegar	1	teaspoon minced garlic
1/4	cup olive oil		

Garnish

edible flowers, fresh basil leaves, chopped fresh chives

Whisk all ingredients for dressing in small bowl. Drizzle on salad just before serving. Decorate with edible flowers, fresh basil leaves or chopped fresh chives.

Serves 4 to 6

Note: This is such a colorful salad for spring or summer. Perfect for picnics, and dressing the salad just before ready to serve keeps it from getting soggy.

Oriental Chicken Noodle Salad

1 pound imported linguine, cooked "al dente," drained and rinsed under cold water

1 1/2 to 2 pounds boneless, skinless chicken breasts, poached, cut into 1-inch pieces

2 cups frozen petite peas, thawed

1 carrot, peeled and cut into julienne strips

1 red pepper, cored and cut into julienne strips

4 green onions, thinly sliced on diagonal

In a large mixing bowl, combine the linguine, chicken, peas, carrot, red pepper and green onions.

Dressing

1/2 cup soy sauce

1/4 cup vegetable or canola oil

1/4 cup rice wine vinegar

2 tablespoons dark sesame oil

1 tablespoon minced garlic

2 tablespoons brown sugar

1 tablespoon freshly grated ginger

2 to 3 drops hot chili oil

2 tablespoons toasted white sesame seeds

2 tablespoons black sesame seeds

In a small bowl, whisk the soy sauce, oil, rice wine vinegar, sesame oil, garlic, sugar, ginger and chili oil. Pour over the pasta and toss to combine. Sprinkle on the sesame seeds. Refrigerate until ready to use. Best made several hours before serving.

Serves 6 to 8

Note: This is one of the most popular salads served at Cucina. We have made thousands of pounds of Oriental Chicken Noodle Salad over the years, for everything from weddings to funerals to business luncheons to birthday parties. It will be a favorite of yours, too.

Orzo Pasta Salad with Chicken and Artichokes

1	pound orzo (rice-shaped) pasta	3/4	cup fresh mint leaves, chopped
1/4	cup julienne-cut sun-dried tomatoes	1	cup feta cheese, crumbled
1	tablespoon olive oil	1/2	cup olive oil
4	cups diced cooked chicken	2	tablespoons minced garlic
2	cups (15-ounce can), artichoke hearts, drained and diced zest and juice of 2 lemons	1	teaspoon salt
		1/2	teaspoon ground black pepper

Cook pasta with the sun-dried tomatoes in the water until "al dente." This allows the tomatoes to rehydrate and flavors the pasta at the same time. Drain, rinse the pasta and sun-dried tomatoes with cold water and mix with 1 tablespoon oil. Set aside.

In a mixing bowl, combine chicken, artichoke hearts, lemon zest and juice, mint, feta, olive oil, garlic, salt and pepper. Toss in the pasta with sun-dried tomatoes. Taste for seasoning. Chill the salad for at least 1 hour before serving. This salad tastes best when made several hours ahead.

Serves 6 to 8

Note: This is one of the most popular pasta salads at Cucina. It has been on the menu since the day the doors opened in 1995, and it still is as good as ever!

Tuscan Tuna and Bean Salad

4	cups (two 15-ounce cans) white northern or cannellini beans, drained and rinsed	3	tablespoons extra-virgin olive oil juice and zest of 1 lemon
2	tablespoons chopped red onions	1/4	cup chopped fresh parsley
1	rib celery, finely diced	1	teaspoon dried thyme
1	(6-ounce) can tuna fish, drained	1/4	teaspoon salt
		1/4	teaspoon ground black pepper

Combine all ingredients in medium bowl, toss gently and refrigerate 1 hour before serving.

Serves 6 to 8

Note: This is one of Cucina's signature salads, a recipe I developed when it first opened, and it remains popular today. It is light and refreshing as part of a buffet or on mixed greens for an easy summer dinner.

Shrimp and Artichoke Salad

2 pounds large shrimp (26 to 30 per pound), peeled, deveined and cooked

2 cups canned artichoke hearts, drained and coarsely chopped

1 small red onion, thinly sliced

2 tablespoons capers

1 pound mixed greens

In a mixing bowl, combine shrimp, artichokes, red onion and capers. Spread the greens onto a large serving platter. Set aside.

Dressing

2 tablespoons Dijon mustard

4 anchovy fillets, finely chopped

1/4 cup chopped fresh parsley

1 tablespoon fresh thyme leaves or 1 teaspoon dried thyme

1 tablespoon minced garlic

1/4 cup mayonnaise

juice of 2 lemons

1/4 cup olive oil

1/2 cup canola oil

1/2 teaspoon salt

1/4 teaspoon ground black pepper

Garnish

1 lemon, thinly sliced

1/4 cup chopped fresh chives

8 sprigs fresh thyme

In a bowl, whisk together the mustard, anchovies, parsley, thyme, garlic, mayonnaise and lemon juice. Whisk in the olive and canola oils just until incorporated. Stir in the salt and pepper. Pour over shrimp mixture. Toss gently. Place on mixed greens and serve at once with lemon slices, chopped chives and thyme sprigs for garnish.

Serves 8 (allowing about 7 shrimp per person)

Note: The shrimp and artichoke salad can be made several hours ahead, then refrigerated until ready to plate on the mixed greens.

Sicilian Seafood Salad

2 quarts water seasoned with 2 bay leaves, 1 teaspoon peppercorns, 1 teaspoon salt

1 1/2 pounds large shrimp (21 to 26 count), raw, peeled and deveined

1 1/2 pounds large scallops (20 to 30 count), raw

1 to 2 pounds calamari (squid), cleaned and cut into 1/2-inch rings, with tentacles

1/2 cup extra-virgin olive oil
juice and zest of 2 lemons

1/4 cup chopped red onion

1/4 cup chopped parsley

1 small red pepper, cored and diced

1 tablespoon minced garlic

1/2 teaspoon salt

1/4 teaspoon ground black pepper

Optional ingredients:

2 ribs celery, diced

1 small fennel bulb, diced

1/4 cup chopped green olives

1/2 teaspoon red pepper flakes

Bring 2 quarts seasoned water to a boil in large saucepan. Add shrimp, scallops and calamari. Cook until shrimp is pink and calamari and scallops are opaque, about 3 minutes. Drain seafood. Transfer to a mixing bowl. Discard peppercorns and bay leaves.

In a separate bowl, whisk together oil, lemon juice and zest, red onion, parsley, red pepper, garlic, salt and pepper. Pour over seafood. Toss well. Cover; refrigerate for at least 1 hour and up to 8 hours before serving chilled.

Serves 6 to 8 as part of a buffet

Note: This recipe is easy to double or triple when serving a crowd. It is always a nice addition to a buffet when a seafood dish is requested.

Soups and Stews

*Savor the Memories of digging for clams and mussels
at low tide in Bayville, Long Island, where we spent a
summer in the perfect summer cottage by the beach...
and of preparing linguini with a spicy red seafood sauce and
sitting at a long oilcloth-covered picnic table.*

Italian Pasta and Bean Soup
(Pasta e Fagioli)

2	tablespoons olive oil		1	teaspoon salt
1	cup diced onion		1/2	teaspoon ground black pepper
2	ribs celery, diced			15-ounce can white northern beans with juice
2	cloves garlic, minced			15-ounce can garbanzo beans with juice
2	cups (15-ounce can) chopped Italian plum tomatoes, with juice		1	cup ditalini (small tubular-shaped) pasta or other small pasta such as shells
6	cups (49-ounce can) chicken broth			
2	large bay leaves			
1	teaspoon dried oregano			

Garnish

1/2	cup grated Romano or Parmesan cheese		1/4	cup chopped fresh parsley

In large stockpot, heat oil. Add onion and celery. Cook 2 minutes on low until soft. Add garlic; cook 1 minute. Add tomatoes, broth, bay leaves, oregano, salt, pepper and the beans. Cover soup; simmer for 30 minutes. Add pasta and cook another 10 minutes. Taste for seasoning. Remove bay leaves before serving. If soup is too thick, thin with a little more broth or water, using 1/2 cup at a time to test the consistency. Serve soup in large bowls with crusty bread and topped with grated cheese and chopped fresh parsley.

Serves 6 to 8

Note: This is one of the most popular soups at Cucina, and can be made in large quantities for large groups by doubling or tripling the recipe. Add 1 cup cooked chicken pieces, 1/4 cup sautéed pancetta or 1/2 pound cooked and crumbled Italian sausage to soup while cooking for added flavor. Perfect for a cold winter's night.

Country-Style Minestrone

4	tablespoons olive oil	1	tablespoon salt
1/4	pound pancetta or bacon, diced	1/2	teaspoon ground black pepper
1	large onion, peeled and diced	1	teaspoon dried basil
1	rib celery, diced	1	teaspoon dried oregano
2	carrots, peeled and diced	1/2	cup dry, small, imported pasta, such as ditali, orzo or elbow
2	tablespoons minced garlic		
1/2	head Savoy cabbage, sliced	2	cups water
1	large baking potato, peeled and diced	1	bunch Swiss chard, cleaned of stems, coarsely chopped, or 1 bunch fresh spinach, cleaned and coarsely chopped
2	cups canned chopped Italian tomatoes		
4	cups (two 15-ounce cans) cannellini or white great northern beans	6	thick slices Italian bread, toasted or grilled
4	cups chicken or vegetable broth	1/4	cup grated Romano cheese

In a large saucepan, heat oil. Add pancetta or bacon and sauté for 3 to 5 minutes until golden brown. Add onion, celery, carrots and garlic. Cook for another minute. Add the cabbage, potato, tomatoes, beans, broth, salt, pepper, basil and oregano. Cover; simmer for 20 minutes. Add pasta and water. Cover and cook another 10 minutes. Stir often to make sure pasta is cooking evenly. Taste for seasoning. Add the Swiss chard, cook another 2 minutes just until wilted. Serve in large soup bowls with a thick slice of bread on bottom of bowl, topped with minestrone and cheese.

Serves 8

Note: This is a thick, hearty soup, filled with vegetables, beans and pasta. It is a great way to feed a large crowd, for it can easily be doubled.

Cucina's Pumpkin Leek Soup

4	tablespoons butter	1/4	teaspoon white pepper
2	large leeks, white part only, cleaned and thinly sliced	2	cups pumpkin purée
2	teaspoons dried thyme	4	cups chicken broth
1/2	teaspoon nutmeg	2	tablespoons brown sugar
1	teaspoon salt	1 1/2	cups half-and-half

Garnish

dollops of sour cream
chopped fresh chives

grated Monterey Jack or white
Cheddar cheese

In a large saucepan, heat butter and sauté the leeks for 8 to 10 minutes on low heat, stirring often. Leeks should be soft and lightly golden. Add the thyme, nutmeg, salt, white pepper, pumpkin purée, chicken broth and brown sugar. Stir, cover and simmer for 15 minutes. Taste for seasoning. Add half-and-half and simmer another 10 minutes. Serve with sour cream, fresh chopped chives and/or grated Monterey Jack or white Cheddar cheese on top.

Serves 6 to 8

We started making this soup in the fall of 1996 at Cucina, and it is featured every day in October and November. Customers never tire of it, request it even after the autumn months and we love to make it for them. It has become synonymous with "Cucina" and "soup" and is a signature dish of ours.

Curried Butternut Squash Soup

4	tablespoons butter	4	cups chicken or vegetable broth
2	pounds butternut or banana squash, peeled, seeded and cut into 1-inch dice	2	teaspoons dried thyme
		2	teaspoons dried oregano
		1	tablespoon curry powder
2	tart apples such as Granny Smith or Pippin, peeled, cored and cut into 1-inch dice	1	cup heavy cream
		1	teaspoon salt
		1/4	teaspoon white pepper
1	large yellow onion, peeled and chopped		

In a medium saucepan, heat butter. Add the cut squash, apples and onion and cook, covered, for 5 minutes, stirring often. Add broth, thyme, oregano and curry powder. Cover, simmer for 15 minutes until squash and apples are soft. Transfer to a food processor or blender, and purée until smooth. Place back in saucepan; add cream, salt and white pepper. Simmer on low heat for 2 to 3 minutes until soup thickens slightly. Taste for seasoning. Serve chilled or warm.

Serves 4 to 6

Note: This soup has always been a favorite at Cucina in the fall, when the squash are at their peak. I like serving it warmed with herbed croutons and shredded white Cheddar cheese on top. A sprig of fresh thyme also adds a nice touch.

Tomato Artichoke Soup

4	tablespoons butter		28-ounce can chopped tomatoes with juices
1	large onion, finely chopped		
1	tablespoon minced garlic	4	cups chicken broth
1	teaspoon dried thyme	1/2	teaspoon salt
	15-ounce can artichoke hearts, coarsely chopped	1/4	teaspoon ground black pepper
		1	cup sour cream

In a large saucepan, heat butter and sauté the onion for 5 minutes until soft. Add the garlic and thyme and sauté another minute. Add the artichoke hearts, tomatoes, chicken broth, salt and pepper. Cover; simmer for 30 minutes. Add the sour cream, stir well and simmer for 5 more minutes. Taste for seasoning.

Serves 8

Note: When the kitchen is crazy at Cucina (which is almost always), this is the soup of the day because it is quick, tasty and loved by our customers.

Tuscan Bread and Sausage Soup

1/4 cup olive oil	8 cups water (2 quarts)
1 large onion, diced	1 teaspoon dried basil
2 ribs celery, diced	1 teaspoon dried oregano
2 carrots, peeled and diced	1 teaspoon salt
1 green bell pepper, cored and chopped	1/2 teaspoon ground black pepper
2 tablespoons minced garlic	8 cups Italian bread, cut into 1-inch cubes
1 pound mild Italian sausage, casings removed (about 4 sausages) 28-ounce can chopped Italian tomatoes with juices	1/2 cup grated Parmesan or Romano cheese

In large stockpot, heat olive oil. Add onion, celery, carrots and green pepper. Sauté on low heat for 5 minutes. Add garlic and sausage. As sausage cooks, crumble with wooden spoon. Cook until sausage is no longer pink, about 8 minutes. Add the canned tomatoes, water, basil, oregano, salt and pepper. Cover; simmer for 30 minutes. While soup is simmering, toast bread cubes on a baking sheet in 375-degree oven for 10 minutes. Allow bread to sit out on baking sheet for a few minutes to harden after removing from oven. Add the toasted bread to the soup after it has simmered 30 minutes, stir and continue to cook another 10 minutes. Taste for seasonings. Remove soup from heat and stir in the grated cheese. Serve immediately.

Serves 8 to 10

Note: I have made this recipe several times in various cooking classes and have received rave reviews from students who have made it a staple in their homes. It is a winner!

Winter Lentil, Swiss Chard and Italian Sausage Soup

1/4	cup olive oil	1	tablespoon dried thyme
2	ribs celery, diced	1	tablespoon salt
1	large onion, peeled and diced	1	teaspoon ground black pepper
2	carrots, peeled and sliced		28-ounce can chopped Italian
2	tablespoons minced garlic		tomatoes with juices
1	pound bulk Italian sausage (hot or sweet)	1	bunch red or green chard, washed and ends trimmed, coarsely chopped
3	cups dry lentils	1/2	cup grated Romano cheese
8	cups chicken broth		

In a large saucepan, heat oil. Sauté the celery, onion and carrots for about 5 minutes or until soft. Add garlic and sausage. Sauté for another 5 to 10 minutes or until sausage is browned and crumbled (crumble with wooden spoon as you cook it). Add the lentils, broth, thyme, salt, pepper and tomatoes. Cover; simmer for 1 hour on low heat, stirring occasionally. Taste for tenderness of lentils and seasoning after 1 hour. If lentils are cooked through, add chard. Cover; simmer for another 5 minutes. If soup is too thick, thin with a little water or more broth. Serve with grated cheese on top and crusty bread.

Serves 6 to 8

Note: Try this dish with pink or green lentils. If Swiss chard is not available in your market, you may substitute 2 bunches of fresh spinach, washed and trimmed. To make it a vegetarian dish, you can omit the sausage.

Chicken and Sausage Jambalaya

8	skinless boneless chicken thighs		2	cups chicken broth
1/2	pound ham, cut into 1/2-inch pieces		2	cups canned chopped tomatoes
1	pound andouille sausage or other smoked sausage, cut into 1-inch pieces		1/4	teaspoon cayenne pepper
			1	tablespoon chili powder
2	tablespoons olive oil		1/4	cup chopped fresh parsley
4	cups water		1	tablespoon dried thyme
2	tablespoons olive oil		1	tablespoon Worcestershire sauce
2	large onions, diced		1	teaspoon Tabasco or other hot sauce
4	ribs celery, diced		1	teaspoon salt
2	green peppers, cored and diced		1	cup converted long grain white rice
4	tablespoons minced garlic			
	8-ounce can tomato paste			

In a medium saucepan or sauté pan, brown the chicken, ham and sausage in 2 tablespoons olive oil for 8 to 10 minutes, turning often so all sides of meat are browned. Add water; cover and simmer for 20 minutes or until chicken is tender. Set aside.

While chicken, ham and sausage are cooking, heat another saucepan with remaining olive oil. Add onions, celery and green peppers. Cook on low heat until onions are soft, about 10 minutes. Add garlic. Cook another minute. Add reserved chicken, ham, sausage, cooking liquid, tomato paste, chicken broth, canned tomatoes, cayenne pepper, chili powder, parsley, thyme, Worcestershire sauce, Tabasco sauce and salt. Cover and simmer for 30 minutes. Add rice; cook another 20 minutes until rice is tender. Taste for seasoning. Total cooking time should be about 1 hour.

Serves 8

Harvest Pork and Yam Stew

$1/4$	cup olive oil		2	parsnips, peeled and sliced thin
1	large onion, diced		1	teaspoon salt
4	ribs celery, sliced		$1/2$	teaspoon ground black pepper
2	carrots, peeled and sliced		1	tablespoon dried sage or $1/4$ cup
1	tablespoon minced garlic			chopped fresh sage leaves
2	pounds boneless lean pork loin, cut		2	cups frozen peas, thawed
	into 1-inch cubes			10-inch round pumpkin, carved out
$1/2$	cup flour			for soup "tureen," optional
4	cups beef or chicken broth		$1/4$	cup chopped fresh parsley
4	cups (approximately 2 pounds)			
	peeled yams, cut into 1-inch cubes			

In a large stockpot, heat olive oil. Add onion, celery and carrots and sauté until soft, about 5 minutes. Add garlic and cubed pork and sauté until pork is browned on all sides. Add flour, stir well to coat meat and cook another minute on medium heat. Add broth, yams, parsnips, salt, pepper and sage. Stir. Cover; simmer on low heat for 30 minutes, stirring occasionally to prevent the stew from sticking to bottom of pot. Taste for seasoning; add peas and cook another 2 minutes. Serve in carved-out 10-inch diameter pumpkin with chopped parsley on top.

Can be made earlier in the day up to the point of adding the peas, which should be added after reheating and just before serving.

Serves 8

Note: This is a perfect autumn evening dinner to serve on Halloween night, when you need to prepare food for a crowd of trick or treaters. Serve with Blueberry Corn Bread (page 33) and Cucina's Festive Mixed Greens (page 39) for a complete meal.

Seafood and Okra Gumbo

1	stick butter (4 ounces)	2	ribs celery, sliced on diagonal
2	large onions, peeled and chopped	1	green pepper, cored and cut into thin strips
3/4	cup flour		
	16-ounce bottle clam juice	4	cups chopped frozen okra, thawed
2	cups canned chopped tomatoes	2	pounds raw large shrimp (21 to 26 per pound), peeled and deveined
1	bay leaf		
1	teaspoon Worcestershire sauce	1	pound raw oysters, drained of their liquor
1	teaspoon salt		
1	teaspoon dried thyme	4	to 6 cups cooked white long grain rice
1	teaspoon sugar		

Garnish

1/4 cup chopped fresh parsley   1/4 cup chopped green onions

In a large saucepan, melt butter. Add chopped onions and sauté until onions are soft and translucent, about 5 minutes on medium heat. Sprinkle flour over onions and butter, cooking on low heat and stirring often for 15 minutes, or until flour has browned. Add clam juice, tomatoes, bay leaf, Worcestershire sauce, salt, thyme, sugar, celery, green pepper and okra. Cover; simmer for 15 minutes. Add shrimp and oysters. Cook for 5 to 8 minutes or until shrimp are pink and oysters are cooked through, but not overdone. Serve in large bowls over cooked rice and garnish with chopped parsley and green onions on top.

Serves 8

Vegetables, Side Dishes, Sauces and Marinades

Savor the Memories of the family piling into our Buick on Friday
nights and driving with the windows down on a summer evening...
to eat scunghilli in spicy tomato sauce over spaghetti and
thick, rich Sicilian-style pizza at The Spumoni Gardens
near Coney Island, under a string of lights.

Fried Artichoke Hearts

2	(10-ounce) packages frozen artichoke hearts, thawed, or 1 can artichoke hearts, drained		2	cups seasoned bread crumbs
			1/4	cup grated Romano cheese
1	cup flour		1/2	teaspoon salt
2	large eggs, beaten		1/4	teaspoon paprika
			1	cup vegetable or canola oil

Pat the artichokes dry with paper towels. Dredge each artichoke heart in flour, in beaten eggs, then in seasoned bread crumbs mixed with cheese, salt and paprika. Set aside until all artichokes are breaded. Heat oil in large skillet and fry artichokes, a few at a time, until golden brown on all sides. Remove to a paper towel-lined platter. Serve with Lemon Oregano Mayonnaise.

Serves 4

Lemon Oregano Mayonnaise

	zest of 1 lemon		1	cup mayonnaise
1	tablespoon chopped fresh oregano or 1 teaspoon dried oregano		1/4	cup heavy cream
			1	teaspoon minced garlic

In blender or food processor, combine all ingredients. Pulse on and off until combined. Do not overblend. Serve on the side with Fried Artichoke Hearts.

Makes about 1 1/2 cups

Note: I had these little gems in Tuscany in May, when fresh baby artichokes were in season, fell in love with them, then created this recipe at home with artichokes available year round.

Sicilian Stuffed Artichokes

4	large artichokes, cleaned according to directions below	1	lemon, cut in half
		4	cups water

Stuffing

3	tablespoons butter	1/4	cup grated Romano cheese
3	tablespoons olive oil	1	teaspoon salt
2	large cloves minced garlic	1	tablespoon olive oil
2	cups dry bread crumbs	1	lemon, cut into 4 slices
1	tablespoon dried Italian seasoning or 1 teaspoon each of: dried oregano, dried basil, dried thyme		

Place cleaned artichokes in a bowl with lemon halves and their juice and 4 cups water. While artichokes are soaking, make stuffing by heating butter and oil in an 8-inch skillet over medium heat. Add garlic and sauté for 30 seconds. Add bread crumbs and dried seasoning. Stir well; cook on low for 1 minute. Remove from heat and stir in Romano cheese.

Spread the leaves of the artichokes open by banging the chokes upside down on work surface. This also allows the excess water to drain out. Fill the center of each artichoke and the leaves with about 1/2 cup of the filling, using a teaspoon so you can get into each leaf.

Place the artichokes in a deep pot wide enough to hold all four artichokes upright. Pour water halfway up the sides of the chokes, add salt and 1 tablespoon olive oil and top each artichoke with one lemon slice. Cover the pot, bring to a boil, then lower heat to a simmer. Cook for 45 minutes, checking to make sure water does not evaporate (add more, if it does). Artichokes should be tender. Remove from heat and serve at room temperature as a first course.

Serves 4

To Buy and Clean Artichokes

Look for tight leaves that are bright green when buying artichokes. Use within 1 day of purchase for they dry out and toughen as they sit in the refrigerator. Cut off the stem just at the base so they can stand upright. Remove the bottom layer of leaves. They are the toughest. Cut off 1/2 inch from the top of the artichoke and with kitchen shears, cut off the prickly tips of each remaining leaf. Remove the center "choke" with a grapefruit spoon. After cleaning each artichoke, place in the acidulated water (bowl with lemon halves and its juice and water). This is a labor intensive process, so don't rush the procedure.

Asparagus Bundles with Tomato Vinaigrette

1   pound fresh asparagus, trimmed to 5-inch lengths (24 spears)

1/2   pound fresh green beans, trimmed (18 beans)

2   carrots, peeled and cut into 5×1/2-inch sticks (12 pieces)

6   green onions, root end trimmed

In 1 quart boiling water with 1 tablespoon salt, blanch asparagus for 2 minutes. Remove asparagus from water and place in iced water to stop cooking process. In same cooking water add the beans and carrots and cook for 4 minutes or until beans are bright green then remove with slotted spoon to iced water. Blanch the green onions in the same cooking water. Drain off excess ice and water from vegetables.

Take 4 asparagus spears, 3 beans and 2 carrot pieces and tie together with one green onion. Do this 6 times. Set aside. You should have 6 bundles.

Vinaigrette

2   Roma tomatoes, finely chopped

1/4   cup chopped fresh mint

1   clove garlic, minced

1/4   cup olive oil

2   tablespoons balsamic vinegar

1/2   teaspoon salt

1/4   teaspoon black pepper

In a medium bowl, mix together the tomatoes, mint, garlic, olive oil, vinegar, salt and pepper.

Garnish

1/4   cup toasted pine nuts

2   tablespoons chopped fresh mint

6   colorful pansies from your garden

When ready to serve asparagus bundles, place on serving platter and top with vinaigrette and sprinkle with pine nuts, chopped mint and pansies for garnish.

Serves 6

Note: This is such a colorful and delicious spring vegetable dish which combines colors, textures and flavors. I have served the bundles with salmon, lamb and roasted chicken.

Eggplant Parmigiana

2	medium eggplant		2	cups Basic Tomato Sauce (page 84)
3	large eggs		1	pound fresh mozzarella, thinly sliced
2	cups seasoned bread crumbs		1/2	cup grated Parmesan cheese
1/2	to 1 cup vegetable oil		1	tablespoon dried oregano

Trim off the ends and tops of the eggplant and slice them into 1/2-inch thick circles. You should have about 16 pieces. Beat the eggs in a shallow dish. Place the bread crumbs on waxed paper or foil. Dip the eggplant slices in the beaten eggs and then into the bread crumbs. Heat 1/2 cup vegetable oil in a large skillet. Fry the eggplant slices over medium-high heat, about 4 at a time until golden on both sides. It is not necessary to cook the eggplant through, because they will be baked further to finish the cooking process. Add more oil to pan, if necessary. Place the fried eggplant slices on paper towels to absorb excess oil. When they have all been fried, lay 8 slices in a shallow baking pan. Top with 1 cup of the tomato sauce, 1/2 of the sliced mozzarella, 1/2 of the grated Parmesan cheese and sprinkle on 1/2 of the dried oregano. Top with 8 more slices of eggplant, trying to fit the same size eggplant over the bottom slices. Top with remaining sauce, mozzarella, Parmesan cheese and oregano. Bake, uncovered, in a 350-degree oven for 25 to 30 minutes until bubbly.

Serves 8

Note: This can be assembled several hours ahead, then covered and refrigerated until ready to bake.

Minty Green Beans with Nuts

2	pounds fresh green beans, cleaned		1	tablespoon chopped garlic
	water		2	tablespoons chopped fresh mint
1	teaspoon salt		1/2	cup toasted chopped hazelnuts,
2	tablespoons olive oil			almonds or walnuts
1	shallot, peeled and chopped			

Place beans and enough water to cover in saucepan and add salt. Cover; bring to a boil, then lower heat to a simmer and cook 5 minutes or until bright green. Drain. In same saucepan, heat oil. Add shallot, garlic and mint. Sauté 1 minute on medium heat. Add drained beans and cook for 1 minute or until beans are heated through. Serve at once with toasted nuts sprinkled on top.

Serves 4 to 6

Note: This is a wonderful vegetable served with lamb, chicken or grilled pork.

Creamed Onions with Parmesan Cheese, Mushrooms and Chives

1/2 stick (2 ounces) butter
1/2 cup flour
1 1/2 cups milk (whole)
1/2 stick (2 ounces) butter
1/2 pound baby button mushrooms
1/2 teaspoon salt

1/4 teaspoon ground black pepper
1/8 teaspoon ground nutmeg
1   bag frozen pearl onions, thawed
1/2 cup shredded Parmesan cheese
1/4 cup chopped fresh chives, fresh
     parsley or thinly sliced green onions

In medium saucepan, heat the 1/2 stick butter until melted. Add flour and stir for 1 minute. Whisk in milk and whisk until thickened, about 2 to 3 minutes on medium heat. In another skillet, heat remaining 1/2 stick butter. Add mushrooms and sauté for 2 minutes, stirring until mushrooms have cooked lightly. Add salt, pepper, nutmeg, pearl onions and sautéed mushrooms to the cream sauce and cook for 2 minutes. Transfer to a 2-quart baking dish, sprinkle with cheese and chives. Bake, covered with foil, for 30 minutes or until bubbly.

Serves 8

Onion and Potato au Gratin

8   Yukon gold or new potatoes (about
     2 pounds)
1   large yellow onion
4   tablespoons butter
1   cup half-and-half

1/2 teaspoon salt
1/2 teaspoon ground black pepper
1   teaspoon dried thyme
1   cup fresh bread crumbs mixed with
     1/2 cup grated Romano cheese

Thinly slice potatoes and onion on mandoline or in food processor. With 1 tablespoon of the butter, rub the bottom and sides of a 2-quart baking dish. Alternate layers of sliced potato and onion. Top with dollops of remaining butter, pour on half-and-half and sprinkle with salt, pepper and thyme. Cover with foil and bake in 375-degree oven for 45 minutes. Remove foil. Top with 1 cup fresh bread crumbs mixture. Bake an additional 10 minutes or until crumbs are browned. Serve warm.

Serves 6 to 8

Potato and Artichoke au Gratin

1/4 cup olive oil
4 large Yukon gold potatoes (about 2 pounds), thinly sliced
1 large Vidalia, Walla Walla or other sweet yellow onion, peeled and thinly sliced
1 can (15-ounce) artichoke hearts, drained, or 10-ounce box frozen artichoke hearts (thawed), coarsely chopped (Do not use marinated artichokes.)

1 teaspoon salt
1/4 teaspoon ground black pepper
1 teaspoon dried thyme
1 cup grated or shredded Parmesan cheese
1 cup half-and-half

Drizzle about 2 tablespoons olive oil on bottom of 2-quart baking dish. Place 1/2 the sliced potatoes in an even layer on bottom. Top with 1/2 the onion and 1/2 the artichokes. Drizzle on remaining oil, sprinkle with a little salt, pepper, 1/2 teaspoon thyme and 1/2 cup grated cheese. Continue with remaining potatoes, onion, artichokes, salt, pepper, thyme and cheese. Pour the half-and-half over the potato layers. Cover with foil; bake at 375 degrees for 1 hour. Remove foil and bake for 5 minutes to brown the top slightly. Serve at once.

Serves 6 to 8

Honey-Spiced Autumn Squash

2 large butternut squash or 4 pounds banana squash, peeled and diced into 1-inch pieces to measure 6 cups cut squash
2 tablespoons butter

1/4 cup honey
1 teaspoon cinnamon
1 teaspoon grated fresh gingerroot
1/2 teaspoon ground cloves
1 teaspoon salt

Place peeled and diced squash in pot with enough water to cover. Bring to boil. Reduce heat to a simmer and cook for 5 minutes. Drain. Cool slightly. Place squash in bowl with remaining ingredients and pour into a greased 2-quart baking dish. (Can be done a day ahead.) Bake, covered, for 20 minutes at 350 degrees; uncover and bake an additional 5 minutes.

Serves 8

Note: When pomegranates are in season (September to January), just before serving, sprinkle the squash with 1/4 cup fresh pomegranate seeds for a colorful visual effect and to add a crunch to the dish.

Polenta-Stuffed Acorn Squash

4	medium acorn squash		2	large whole eggs
2	cups water		2	large egg yolks
$1/2$	teaspoon salt		$1/4$	cup grated Romano cheese
1	cup polenta or yellow cornmeal		1	teaspoon dried basil
2	tablespoons butter		1	pomegranate, seeded, if in season

Trim ends of acorn squash so they can stand upright, then cut in half horizontally and scoop out the seeds. Place the 8 halves in a baking dish with cut sides down, add enough water to come $1/2$ up sides of squash and bake, uncovered, in a 375-degree oven for 30 minutes. Remove squash from oven, drain off water and turn squash halves upright.

While squash are baking, make polenta stuffing. In a medium saucepan, bring the 2 cups water and salt to a boil, and slowly add the polenta, whisking until thickened. Cook on low heat for 3 to 4 minutes, stirring often. Remove from heat. Whisk in the butter, the whole eggs and egg yolks, cheese and basil. Fill the center of each squash with about $1/4$ cup of the polenta mixture. Add enough water to pan to reach 1 inch up sides of squash and return to oven and bake for 20 to 25 minutes until polenta is puffed and squash is golden. Remove from oven, sprinkle each squash with pomegranate seeds and serve at once.

Serves 8

Note: I love making this dish in the fall as an accompaniment to turkey, pork or just as a first course. It is eye-catching and delicious, not to mention fairly easy to assemble.

Pan-Fried Tomatoes with Spinach and Pine Nuts

2	pounds fresh spinach leaves	1/2	teaspoon salt
2	tablespoons olive oil	1/4	teaspoon black pepper
2	cloves garlic, minced	1/4	cup toasted pine nuts
1/4	teaspoon nutmeg	2	tablespoons extra-virgin olive oil
1	pint container cherry, baby red pear or grape tomatoes		

Rinse spinach leaves and shake off excess water. In a medium saucepan, heat oil. Add garlic and sauté 1 minute on low heat. Add spinach and nutmeg and cook until spinach is wilted, about 2 minutes. Remove spinach to a bowl. Add the tomatoes to saucepan and cook on high heat just to heat through. Toss in salt, pepper and pine nuts. Add spinach back to pan and cook an additional minute. Entire cooking process should take no more than 5 minutes. Serve at once with extra-virgin olive oil drizzled on top.

Serves 4

Note: This is a wonderful side dish to roast pork with rosemary or to pork tenderloins and fennel.

Brandied Yam Soufflé

3	pounds yams, peeled, cut into 2-inch pieces	4	egg yolks
1/2	stick (2 ounces) butter	1	teaspoon salt
1/4	cup brown sugar	1/2	teaspoon ground nutmeg
	zest and juice of 1 orange	1/4	cup brandy, rum or bourbon
		4	egg whites

Cook the yams until tender then drain. Place in mixing bowl of mixer fit with paddle. Beat until smooth, about 1 minute on medium speed. Add the butter, brown sugar, zest and juice of the orange, 4 egg yolks, salt, nutmeg and brandy. Beat another 2 minutes on medium speed. (Can be made ahead up to this point, then refrigerated.) In a separate bowl, beat egg whites until stiff peaks form. Fold the beaten egg whites into the yam mixture. Do not overmix. Pour into a buttered 2-quart soufflé dish or decorative 3-inch deep baking dish. Bake at 400 degrees for 25 to 30 minutes or until puffed and golden.

Serves 8 to 10

Note: This is a very rich side dish and can be served in small portions.
It is a staple at our Thanksgiving table every year.

End of Summer Ratatouille

Dressing

1	bunch fresh parsley, coarsely chopped
1	red onion, thinly sliced
4	cloves garlic, slivered

1	tablespoon kosher salt
1	teaspoon ground black pepper
1/2	cup olive oil

Vegetable Layer

1/4	cup olive oil
1	medium eggplant, diced into 1-inch cubes
2	yellow squash, diced into 1-inch cubes
2	zucchini, diced into 1-inch cubes
1	red bell pepper, diced into 1-inch cubes

1	yellow bell pepper, diced into 1-inch cubes
1	green bell pepper, diced into 1-inch cubes
3	large ripe tomatoes, coarsely chopped

Topping

1/2	cup chopped fresh basil leaves

8-ounce log Montrachet, goat cheese or chèvre cheese, or 1 cup grated Parmesan cheese

In a small bowl, combine parsley, red onion, garlic, kosher salt, pepper and olive oil.

In a medium skillet, heat oil. Sauté eggplant until soft, about 2 minutes, stirring often. Transfer eggplant and oil from pan to decorative 4-quart baking dish. Layer vegetables in order given, with a little of the dressing mixture in between each layer. Finish with tomatoes on top. Cover with foil. Bake at 350 degrees for 30 minutes. Remove foil and top with basil and cheese. Bake, uncovered, for an additional 5 minutes to melt cheese.

Serves 8

Our Traditional Italian Sausage Stuffing

The night before stuffing the bird, prepare stuffing. This recipe makes enough to stuff a 22- to 25-pound turkey, with ample left over to bake separately.

8	quarts cubed loaves of bread, such as sliced white sandwich, foccacia, ciabatta (about 3 pounds bread)	4	tablespoons dried oregano
		2	tablespoons fennel seeds
		1	tablespoon coarsely ground pepper
2	sticks butter	2	pounds bulk Italian sausage
2	large onions, diced	2	quarts whole milk

Bake bread on baking sheet in 200-degree oven for 10 to 15 minutes or until dry, not toasted. Toss bread cubes occasionally to get the heat throughout the bread. Set aside in a 13-quart bowl. In a large saucepan, melt butter. Sauté onions until soft, about 10 minutes. Add dried oregano, fennel seeds and coarsely ground pepper. Cook another 4 to 5 minutes on low heat. Add bread cubes to onions and mix well. Cook on low heat, stirring often, until bread has been coated with the butter-onion mixture. Transfer the bread cubes to the 13-quart bowl. In same pot, brown Italian sausage until cooked through, crumbling the sausage as you cook it. Transfer the sausage to bowl with bread. Mix all ingredients well. The bread should be coated with sausage and onions. Taste for seasoning. Refrigerate stuffing until ready to use. When ready to stuff bird, add enough whole milk to bread stuffing to soften (about 6 to 8 cups of milk, depending on density of bread). Don't make it soggy. Stuff cavities of bird loosely and put remaining stuffing in baking pan. Bake extra stuffing at 350 degrees for 30 minutes, covered with foil.

Serves 12 to 15

Basil and Tomato Rice Pilaf

2	tablespoons butter	1	cup chopped fresh tomatoes
1/2	cup capellini or vermicelli pasta, broken into 1-inch pieces	2	cups chicken broth
		1/2	teaspoon salt
1	tablespoon chopped onion	1/4	teaspoon ground black pepper
1	cup raw converted rice	2	tablespoons chopped fresh basil

In a medium saucepan, heat butter and sauté the pasta until golden brown, about 3 minutes on low heat. Add the onion and cook another minute. Add rice, tomatoes, broth, salt and pepper. Cover; simmer for 15 minutes until rice is tender. Allow to sit off the heat for 5 minutes, then stir in the fresh basil.

Serves 4

Arancini (Italian Stuffed Rice Balls)

2	tablespoons butter		1	large egg
1/4	cup chopped onion		1/4	cup bread crumbs
1 1/2	cups arborio rice			pinch of salt and pepper
4	cups chicken broth		4	ounces fresh mozzarella, cut into
1/2	cup tomato sauce			1/2-inch cubes
1/2	cup grated Romano or Parmesan cheese		2	to 3 cups fine dried bread crumbs
1/2	cup peas		2	to 3 cups vegetable oil for frying

In a medium saucepan, heat butter and sauté onion until soft. Add rice, stir well. Add broth, one cup at a time, stirring until broth is absorbed, and continue to add more broth, stirring until absorbed. After 15 to 20 minutes, rice should be cooked but tender. Remove from heat. Cool to room temperature. Transfer to a bowl and add tomato sauce, cheese, peas, egg and 1/4 cup bread crumbs. Add a pinch of salt and pepper.

Scoop about 2 tablespoons rice mixture in left hand, make a well in center, add a cube of mozzarella, top with more rice to form a ball about 2 inches in diameter. Roll in dried bread crumbs. Place on platter and continue to make rice balls until all rice is used. Heat oil to 375 degrees. Add balls to oil, 2 at a time, frying until golden brown and turning to cook evenly. This should take about 4 to 5 minutes. Remove with slotted spoon to paper-lined plate. Serve immediately.

Makes about 12 to 15 balls

Note: Arancini, or rice balls, are served with marinara sauce, if desired. Since they are round and look like oranges, they are called arancini or "orange" in Italian. They have been in Italian delicatessens for years and are now making a resurgence in popularity in gourmet stores around the country.

Risotto Primavera (Springtime Risotto)

2 tablespoons olive oil
1/2 cup chopped onions
1 1/2 cups arborio rice
1/2 teaspoon saffron threads
5 to 6 cups (49-ounce can works well) warmed chicken broth
1 cup frozen petite peas, thawed
1 carrot, peeled and finely diced
1 pound asparagus, tough ends trimmed, blanched and cut into 1-inch pieces
1/4 cup chopped fresh chives
1/2 cup grated Romano cheese
2 tablespoons butter
2 tablespoons chopped fresh chives

In a medium saucepan, heat olive oil and sauté onions until soft and translucent, about 5 minutes over medium heat. Add rice; stir well to coat rice with oil and onions. Add saffron threads to broth to dissolve. Lower heat, and add 1 cup of the broth to rice mixture; stir well to allow the broth to be absorbed while cooking on low heat. Continue to add the broth, one cup at a time until all the broth is incorporated into the rice and rice is tender. This process will take about 25 to 30 minutes. Add peas, carrot, asparagus and 1/4 cup chives to rice, and cook on low heat until vegetables are warmed through, about 5 minutes. Remove from heat and stir in the Romano cheese and butter. Rice should be creamy, not liquid. At this point you may have to add a little salt and pepper, if desired. Serve at once with 2 tablespoons chives as garnish.

Serves 4

Cilantro Butter

4 ounces (1 stick) butter, softened
1 tablespoon minced garlic
1/2 cup chopped fresh cilantro
1/2 jalapeño pepper, cored and chopped
1/8 teaspoon paprika
1 shallot, peeled and coarsely chopped
1/4 teaspoon white pepper

In a food processor, combine all ingredients and blend until smooth, about 1 minute. With a spatula, remove from work bowl, place on plastic wrap and roll into a log, 1 inch wide and 5 inches long. Wrap in plastic and chill until ready to use. Cut into thin slices, and use on grilled pork chops, salmon, grilled chicken, grilled turkey breasts or grilled vegetables.

Makes about 1 cup butter

Note: This butter freezes well.

Cilantro Pesto

1 cup chopped fresh cilantro
$^1/_2$ cup chopped fresh parsley
juice of 1 lime
2 tablespoons minced garlic
1 teaspoon salt

$^1/_2$ teaspoon ground black pepper
$^1/_2$ cup toasted pine nuts
$^1/_2$ cup grated Romano cheese
$^3/_4$ cup olive oil

Place cilantro, parsley, lime juice, garlic, salt, pepper, pine nuts and cheese in food processor. With motor running slowly add the olive oil. Mixture should be thick and bright green. Remove from food processor and refrigerate until ready to use. Use it as a base for cilantro pesto mayonnaise, toss in pasta salad, brush on salmon or chicken. It is best used within 2 days.

Makes about 1$^1/_2$ cups pesto

Pear Ginger Chutney

2 tablespoons butter
2 pears, cored and chopped
$^1/_2$ cup golden raisins
1 tablespoon freshly grated ginger
$^1/_4$ cup sugar

1 cup orange juice
zest of 1 orange
$^1/_4$ teaspoon cinnamon
$^1/_4$ teaspoon ground nutmeg

In small saucepan, heat butter. Add chopped pears, raisins and ginger. Sauté for 2 minutes or until pears are soft. Add sugar, orange juice, orange zest, cinnamon and nutmeg. Cover; cook on low for 5 minutes. Remove from heat. Cool.

Makes about 2 cups

Note: This is a zesty accompaniment to lamb, pork or poultry. Best made a day or two in advance, then chilled until ready to serve.

Spiced Cranberry Orange Relish

12-ounce bag fresh cranberries
1 cup water
1 cup sugar
1 apple (Pippin, Granny Smith or Golden Delicious), cored and cut into 1/2-inch dice
1 pear (Comice, D'Anjou or Bosc), cored and cut into 1/2-inch dice
zest and juice of 1 orange
1/4 teaspoon of each: ground cinnamon, ground cloves, ground nutmeg
2 tablespoons orange liqueur (optional)

In a medium saucepan, bring the cranberries, water and sugar to a boil. Lower heat to a simmer; add apple, pear, orange zest, orange juice and spices. Simmer for 10 minutes until cranberries pop. Cool relish to room temperature. Refrigerate relish until ready to serve. Stir in the orange liqueur just before serving. Can be made several days in advance.

Serves 6 to 8

Note: Serve with turkey, chicken, pork or duck. Delicious warmed over ice cream!

Roquefort Horseradish Rosemary Sauce

4 ounces Roquefort cheese
1/4 cup prepared bottled horseradish
16 ounces (1 pint) sour cream
1 tablespoon fresh rosemary leaves
2 sprigs fresh rosemary and 4 whole fresh cranberries, garnish

Combine Roquefort, horseradish, sour cream and rosemary leaves in food processor or blender. Purée until well blended and smooth. Transfer to bowl, cover and chill until ready to serve. (Can be made a day ahead.) Garnish sauce with rosemary sprigs and cranberries when ready to serve.

Makes 2 cups

Note: This is a perfect sauce for oven-roasted beef tenderloin or grilled New York, rib eye or fillet mignon steaks. Serve it on crusty rolls for roast beef sandwiches, too.

Grandpa's Tomato Mint Sauce

1   tablespoon kosher salt
2   large cloves garlic, cut in half
1/4 cup fresh mint leaves
2   large ripe tomatoes, cored and cut
     into quarters

1/4 teaspoon ground black pepper
1/2 cup extra-virgin olive oil

In a mortar and pestle or with a wooden spoon in a small bowl, combine the salt and garlic. Grind the garlic, using the pestle or the back of the wooden spoon, until the garlic is almost a purée. This takes a little "elbow grease," but the garlic will eventually become soft. Add the mint and crush the leaves with the pestle until fragrant. Add the cut tomatoes and again, with the pestle, crush the tomatoes until they are incorporated into the garlic and mint. Crush in the pepper and then add the olive oil until all the ingredients are incorporated into a sauce. (This entire process takes about 10 minutes, so don't lose your patience.) Taste for seasoning. Use the tomato mint sauce on grilled chicken, steaks or lamb.

Makes about 1 cup sauce

Note: If you don't have a mortar and pestle, or the time, the process can be done in a food processor, but the texture will be different. The flavors are still wonderful, though!

Lemon Herb Marinade

    zest and juice of 2 lemons
1   large onion, peeled and thinly sliced
1/2 cup olive oil
2   tablespoons minced garlic
1   teaspoon kosher salt
1/2 teaspoon ground black pepper
1   tablespoon dried thyme or
     3 tablespoons chopped fresh
     thyme leaves

1   tablespoon dried rosemary or
     3 tablespoons chopped fresh
     rosemary
10 juniper berries, crushed
1   tablespoon fennel seeds

Combine all ingredients in a nonmetallic bowl. Use as a marinade for chicken, pork, lamb, turkey breasts, sea bass, halibut, scallops, shrimp and salmon.

Makes about 1 1/2 cups marinade

Entrées

Savor the Memories of August nights in Brooklyn,
walking with friends to attend the religious feasts
on the streets around St. Rosalia's Church...
where zeppole (deep-fried dough topped with powdered sugar),
Italian sausage, pepper and onion sandwiches, and
torrone nougat candy were reasons for fighting the crowds.

Standing Rib Roast with Yorkshire Pudding

	5- to 6-pound small end rib roast	kosher salt
	with bone in, trimmed of excess fat	coarsely ground black pepper
2	cloves garlic, cut in half	

Place beef, bone end down, in a roasting pan. Rub the outer surface with garlic. Sprinkle lightly with kosher salt and black pepper. Roast in a preheated 450-degree oven for 15 minutes, tenting with foil to prevent splattering in the oven. Reduce heat to 325 degrees, remove the foil and roast for 15 minutes per pound, testing for doneness. The roast should read 135 to 140 degrees on a meat thermometer for medium-rare. Remove from oven and allow roast to "rest" about 15 minutes before slicing. The roast will continue to "cook" a little more as it is resting because the bones are conducting heat. Bake the Yorkshire Pudding while roast is resting.

Optional: After the roast has cooked, remove roast from pan to a warm platter and deglaze the pan. Remove the excess fat from roasting pan, and over medium heat add 1 cup red wine and 1 cup water. With a wooden spoon, scrape the pan drippings and cook for 2 minutes. This makes a wonderful "au jus" to serve on top of sliced meat. Taste for seasoning, and add a little salt and pepper if needed. Serve roast with pan drippings and prepared horseradish.

Serves 6 to 8

Yorkshire Pudding

1	cup flour	1 1/4	cups whole milk
1/2	teaspoon salt	1	tablespoon cold water
2	large eggs		

Mix flour and salt in small bowl. With an electric mixer, beat in the eggs, milk and water until batter is smooth. Have this process done before removing beef from oven, so that the roast is not "resting" too long. Drain off about 2 tablespoons fat from roasting pan to an 8-inch round baking dish or cake pan. Place in 400-degree oven for 3 minutes. Remove carefully and add pudding batter. Bake on top shelf of 400-degree oven for 15 minutes or until puffed and golden. Cut into 6 to 8 wedges and serve with roast.

A standing rib roast is one of the easiest dishes to make, an impressive entrée and yet most cooks fear the roasting process. Remember to cook with bones down, sear it first and roast at a fairly low heat until it reaches the proper temperature. Don't try to rush the process. Allow yourself at least 2 hours of cooking time for a 6-pound roast. You can always wait for the roast, but if it is overdone, then there is no going back.

Beef Tenderloin with Green Peppercorn Sauce

	5- to 6-pound beef tenderloin	1	tablespoon cornstarch mixed with
1	tablespoon kosher salt		1 cup beef broth
1	tablespoon coarsely ground black	1/2	cup red wine
	pepper	1	tablespoon canned green
1	tablespoon herbes de Provence		peppercorns
2	tablespoons butter	1	tablespoon chopped fresh rosemary
2	large shallots, chopped	1/2	teaspoon salt

Trim the beef tenderloin by removing the "silver" and excess fat. Mix the salt, pepper and herbes de Provence in a bowl. Rub the entire surface of the beef with the mixture. Preheat the oven to 500 degrees. Place beef in a roasting pan and place in preheated oven for only 10 minutes. Lower the heat to 325 degrees and roast for 10 to 12 minutes per pound for medium-rare. Test with thermometer in thickest part of beef. It should read 115 degrees. Let the roast rest for 10 minutes before slicing.

For Sauce: In small saucepan, heat butter. Add shallots. Sauté for 1 minute. Add the cornstarch and beef broth mixture; cook on medium heat until the sauce has thickened slightly. Add the wine, green peppercorns, rosemary and salt. Cook another minute on low heat. Taste for seasoning. Serve warm over sliced beef with rosemary sprig on top.

Serves 10 to 12

Note: We have made hundreds of these beef tenderloins for parties when catering at Cucina. It is easy, elegant and though expensive, it will feed 10 to 12 people. Perfect for a special dinner party or to serve as part of a buffet.

Corned Beef and Cabbage with Parsley Sauce

	5- to 6-pound corned beef brisket	5	carrots, peeled and quartered
12	peppercorns and 1 tablespoon pickling spice or packaged pickling spices (which come in store-bought corned beef)	3	large onions, peeled and quartered
		2	pounds baby new potatoes
		1	medium cabbage, cut into 6 wedges

Parsley Sauce

2	ounces (1/2 stick) butter	1	teaspoon salt
1/4	cup flour	1/4	teaspoon ground white pepper
1	cup milk	1	cup chopped fresh parsley

In a large stockpot, place corned beef in water to cover by 2 inches along with peppercorns or pickling spices. Cover; bring to boil, reduce heat and simmer for 4 hours or until tender, skimming occasionally.

About 45 minutes before serving, place carrots, onions and potatoes in pot. Cook for 30 minutes or until vegetables are tender. Add cabbage to pot and cook an additional 15 minutes.

While vegetables are cooking, make the parsley sauce. Heat butter in small saucepan. Add flour and whisk for 1 minute. Slowly whisk in milk, salt and pepper. Cook on low heat until sauce thickens. Add parsley; taste for seasoning.

When ready to serve, place meat on platter and slice thin across the grain. Place vegetables around platter and top with parsley sauce. Serve meat with coarse grain mustard and horseradish, if desired.

Serves 6

Note: Corned beef and cabbage is one of the easiest dishes to make and although it is traditionally served around St. Patrick's Day, I enjoy serving it on cold winter nights in January. It is a comfort food, especially with the parsley sauce on top. And it is literally a one-pot dish (except for the sauce, of course).

Braciole (Stuffed Meat Rolls)

1- to 1 1/2-pound top round, cut into 1/8-inch thick slices for "rouladen" or "braciole" (about twelve 6×6-inch slices)
1/2 pound lean ground beef
2 cups dry bread crumbs
2 large eggs
1 tablespoon minced garlic
1/4 cup chopped fresh parsley
1/4 cup golden raisins
1/4 cup toasted pine nuts
1/2 teaspoon salt
1/4 teaspoon ground black pepper
1/2 cup grated Romano cheese
1/4 cup olive oil
4 cups Basic Tomato Sauce (page 84)
1 cup red wine

Lay each slice of beef flat on a work surface. For the filling, combine the ground beef, bread crumbs, eggs, garlic, parsley, raisins, pine nuts, salt, pepper and Romano cheese; mix well. Place 1/4 cup filling in the center of each slice of beef. Roll up jellyroll style and secure with a toothpick. In a large skillet, heat the oil. Add 4 beef rolls at a time, brown on all sides and transfer to a saucepan with the Basic Tomato Sauce and red wine. Simmer for at least 1 hour, covered, stirring often to prevent the sauce from sticking to the pan. Remove the toothpicks and serve the braciole and sauce over pasta, polenta or as an entrée.

Makes about 12 meat rolls

Cucina's Classic Meat Loaf

2 1/2 pounds lean ground beef
2 large eggs
1/2 cup quick-cook oats
1/2 cup ketchup
1 medium onion, chopped
1 teaspoon salt
1/4 teaspoon ground black pepper
2 tablespoons ketchup
2 tablespoons quick-cook oats

Combine the ground beef, eggs, 1/2 cup oats, 1/2 cup ketchup, onion, salt and pepper until well mixed. Press into a 9×5×3-inch loaf pan. Spread with the 2 tablespoons ketchup and sprinkle the 2 tablespoons oats over the top. Bake in a preheated 350-degree oven for 1 hour or until meat thermometer reads 160 degrees. Cut into 1 1/2-inch thick slices.

Serves 6

Note: It has always amazed me that something as simple as meat loaf made so many people happy. Comments such as "just as my mother made" or it is "my comfort food" allow us to serve this dish proudly day after day, especially with our garlic mashed potatoes.

Grandma Rose's Meatballs and Tomato Sauce with Pasta

Meatballs

1	pound ground lean beef	1/4	cup finely chopped parsley
1	pound ground lean pork	1	teaspoon dried Italian seasoning
2	large eggs	2	cups soft bread crumbs
1	tablespoon minced garlic	1/2	cup milk
1/4	cup freshly grated Romano pecorino	1/2	teaspoon salt
	or Parmesan cheese	1/2	teaspoon black pepper

Mix all ingredients in medium bowl until well combined. Use your hands to mix well, then form into 1 1/2-inch balls. Place on a greased baking sheet. You can bake or fry the meatballs at this point, using olive oil to fry them. If baking, bake at 375 degrees for 5 to 8 minutes or until golden brown on outside but not cooked through. If frying, heat 2 tablespoons olive oil in skillet and brown about 10 meatballs per batch, browning on all sides; do not cook through. Place meatballs in prepared sauce to finish cooking.

Makes about 25 meatballs

Note: The trick to tender, soft meatballs is to finish the cooking process in the sauce.

Basic Tomato Sauce

1/4	cup olive oil	1	tablespoon dried Italian seasoning
1	cup chopped onion		(basil, oregano, thyme, parsley)
2	large cloves garlic, minced	1/2	cup red wine
	pinch of red pepper flakes	1/2	teaspoon salt
2	(28-ounce) cans chopped Italian		
	tomatoes in purée		

Heat olive oil in medium saucepan. Add onion and cook for 2 to 3 minutes or until soft. Add garlic and red pepper flakes. Sauté for 1 minute. Add tomatoes, Italian seasoning, wine and salt. Cover; simmer for 30 minutes. Add meatballs and cook an additional 30 minutes on low heat.

Sauce with meatballs can be made a day ahead, then refrigerated. Reheat on low heat, bringing to a simmer slowly. This sauce freezes well, also.

Baked Ziti with Bolognese Sauce

2   pounds imported ziti or penne pasta, cooked a little under "al dente," drained

Bolognese Sauce

¹/4   cup olive oil
1   small onion, finely diced
2   ribs celery, finely diced
2   tablespoons minced garlic
1   pound lean ground beef or veal
1   pound ground pork
2   (28-ounce) cans chopped Italian tomatoes with purée
¹/4   cup finely chopped parsley

2   cups half-and-half
1   cup beef broth
1   teaspoon salt
¹/2   teaspoon ground black pepper
2   pounds whole milk ricotta
1   pound fresh mozzarella, cut into ¹/2-inch cubes
1   cup grated Parmesan or Romano cheese

Cook pasta; set aside.

In a medium saucepan, heat olive oil. Add onion, carrot and celery. Sauté until soft, about 5 minutes. Add garlic and cook another minute. Add ground beef and pork. Cook until no longer pink, crumbling with a wooden spoon as you cook. Add tomatoes, parsley, half-and-half, beef broth and salt. Cover; simmer for 30 minutes. Taste for seasoning. Combine the ricotta, cubed mozzarella and grated cheese in a medium bowl.

To assemble: Place enough of the sauce in the bottom of a 13×9×3-inch baking dish to coat evenly. Add ¹/3 of the cooked pasta, top with more sauce, ¹/3 of the cheese mixture, and continue to assemble until pasta and cheese are used, spooning enough sauce on each layer to cover. You should finish with sauce as top layer. Cover loosely with foil and bake at 375 degrees for 45 minutes. Remove foil and bake an additional 5 minutes. Serve hot.

Serves 8 to 10

Note: This can be assembled earlier in the day, even the day before, then baked. You might have to increase the baking time by 10 minutes if you are taking the ziti out of the refrigerator.

If there is one dish that epitomizes my family dinners, it is Baked Ziti. Layers of tubular-shaped pasta, homemade tomato sauce, fresh whole milk ricotta and mozzarella, grated Romano or Locatelli cheese gently baked until bubbly and served in massive quantities. To this day, my daughter, Sarah, requests this dish at her birthday dinner and parties for friends. I have served it to my son's basketball teams and tennis teams, running friends and at holiday gatherings. It is the essence of southern Italian cooking, the essence of my childhood and the essence of my kitchen.

Crown Roast of Pork with Jeweled Rice Stuffing

1	crown roast of pork, prepared by butcher (16 chops, Frenched and tied)	1	tablespoon dried thyme
		1	tablespoon fennel seeds
1/4	cup olive oil	1	tablespoon kosher salt
2	cloves garlic, minced	1/2	teaspoon ground black pepper

Stuffing

2	cups long grain rice, cooked a little underdone, drained	1	teaspoon salt
		1/2	teaspoon black pepper
1	cup wild rice, cooked a little underdone, drained	2	tablespoons melted butter
		1/2	cup chopped fresh parsley
2	cups packaged chopped dried fruit medley (dried cranberries, raisins, apricots, dates)	1	tablespoon herbes de Provence or Italian seasoning
1	cup pecan or walnut pieces	2	cups beef broth (divided 1 cup and 1 cup)
1	bunch green onions, thinly sliced on diagonal (tops removed)	1	cup red wine

Place the pork roast in baking pan large enough to hold it upright. (You may place it on a rack, too, if you prefer.) In a small bowl, combine the oil, garlic, thyme, fennel, salt and pepper. Rub mixture over the outer side of the roast. In a medium bowl, combine all ingredients for the stuffing. Place stuffing loosely in the center of the roast, filling the center up to the top of the bones. Place any leftovers in baking dish for baking later. Place roast in preheated 325-degree oven and roast in center of oven for 20 minutes. Add 1 cup beef broth and 1 cup red wine. Cover loosely with foil at this point. Add more broth to pan, if drying out. After roasting for 2 hours, test roast with meat thermometer. It should register 170 degrees at the center of the meatiest section when done. Roast should take 15 minutes per pound to cook to that temperature. Heat remaining stuffing during the last 30 minutes of roasting time in 325-degree oven. Allow the roast to rest for 10 minutes before slicing into 8 rib bone sections. Serve stuffing on side. Use pan drippings to make a sauce.

Serves 8, generously

Note: Using rice which is a little undercooked will ensure that the rice will not be overcooked and mushy when baked with the pork.

Stuffed Pork Loin with Apple Mint Chutney

3-	to 4-pound boneless pork loin, trimmed and cut in half horizontally to allow the roast to lay flat (butterflied)	2	carrots, peeled and diced
		2	cups fresh bread crumbs
		1	teaspoon dried thyme
		1	teaspoon salt
2	ounces ($1/2$ stick) butter	$1/2$	teaspoon black pepper
1	medium onion, diced	$1/2$	cup milk or half-and-half
2	ribs celery, diced		

Topping

1	tablespoon kosher salt	6	to 8 sprigs of fresh rosemary, thyme or sage
1	teaspoon coarsely ground black pepper	1	cup chicken or beef broth

Lay pork loin, fat side down, on work surface. Flatten with meat pounder to $1^1/2$-inch thickness. For the stuffing, heat butter in a medium skillet. Sauté onion, celery and carrots in the skillet until soft, about 3 minutes. Remove from heat and stir in bread crumbs, thyme, salt, pepper and milk or half-and-half. Mix well. Spread filling evenly on pork loin. Roll up jelly roll style from wide end. Tie the roast with kitchen string at 2-inch intervals. Season with kosher salt and pepper and tuck the sprigs of herbs under the string on top, and underneath the roast. Roast in a preheated 350-degree oven for about $1^1/2$ hours, depending on size of roast. Add 1 cup chicken broth or beef broth to pan after 30 minutes of roasting. Test for doneness after 1 hour. Internal temperature of roast should be 145 to 150 degrees. Remove from oven and allow to "rest" before slicing and serving with Apple Mint Chutney and pan juices.

Serves 6 to 8

Apple Mint Chutney

2	tablespoons butter	2	tablespoons brown sugar
4	Granny Smith apples, peeled, cored and diced	$1/2$	teaspoon nutmeg juice and zest of 1 lemon
1	small onion, diced	1	cup fresh mint leaves, chopped

In a medium skillet, heat butter. Add the apples and onion and sauté for 5 minutes on low heat. Stir in brown sugar, nutmeg, lemon juice and zest. Cook another 2 to 3 minutes. Remove from heat and stir in fresh mint leaves. Cool. Serve with pork roast.

Makes about 2 cups

Grilled Pork Tenderloins Mediterranean Style on Creamy Polenta and Spinach

	2 to 3 pounds pork tenderloins	2	tablespoons olive oil
1	tablespoon minced garlic	1	bulb fennel, thinly sliced
1	tablespoon fennel seeds	1	small onion, thinly sliced
1	tablespoon mustard seeds	2	cloves garlic, slivered
1	teaspoon kosher salt	1	cup beef broth, chicken broth or
1	teaspoon coarsely ground pepper		red wine
1	tablespoon dried oregano		

Place pork tenderloins on a work surface. In a small bowl, combine 1 tablespoon garlic, fennel seeds, mustard seeds, salt, pepper, oregano and oil. Stir to combine to make a paste. Rub pork on all sides with the mixture. (Can be done up to 24 hours in advance. Refrigerate.)

Heat grill to medium heat. Grill pork on all sides for 3 to 4 minutes per side. Transfer to a baking dish and add the sliced fennel, onion and slivered garlic and bake in preheated 350-degree oven for 20 more minutes. (Total cooking time is about 35 minutes from grill to table.) Deglaze the pan with the broth or wine. Thinly slice pork on diagonal and serve with roasted fennel, onion, garlic and pan juices on top. While pork is baking, make polenta and spinach.

Serves 4

Creamy Polenta

3	cups water (or 2 cups water, 1 cup chicken broth)	2	tablespoons butter
		3/4	cup Parmesan cheese
1	teaspoon salt	2	tablespoons chopped fresh parsley
1	cup polenta or cornmeal		

In a medium saucepan, heat water to a boil. Add salt and slowly add the polenta, stirring as you add. Add butter and Parmesan cheese. Stir constantly until polenta thickens, about 5 minutes. Stir in parsley.

Serves 4

Sautéed Spinach

2	tablespoons olive oil	$1/8$	teaspoon ground nutmeg
2	cloves garlic, slivered	$1/2$	teaspoon salt
1	to $1^{1}/2$ pounds washed spinach leaves (leave water on leaves)	$1/4$	teaspoon ground black pepper

In a large skillet, heat oil. Add garlic and sauté until fragrant, about 1 minute on low heat. Add the washed spinach leaves; stir well and add nutmeg, salt and pepper. Cover and steam for 3 minutes, stirring often. When spinach is just wilted, it is ready to serve. Do not overcook.

Serves 4

To Serve Dish: Place polenta in a large serving platter and top with the sliced pork tenderloins, fennel, onions and garlic with pan juices, in a concentric circle on top. Place the sautéed spinach around the polenta and pork. Drizzle the entire dish with a little extra-virgin olive oil, if desired. Serve at once.

Note: This is the perfect end-of-summer dish. It has the flavors of autumn, yet the grilled pork still reminds us that summer was just here. I have served this dish for many a casual dinner party with end-of-summer sliced yellow and red tomato salad with basil, red onions and goat cheese and a Sour Cream Apple Walnut Pie (page 132) for dessert.

If you are not in the mood for polenta, I have also used lentils as a base for this pork. Pink lentils are especially attractive. You can also try couscous.

Spaghetti alla Carbonara

1	pound imported spaghetti, cooked "al dente," drained		2	egg yolks
1/4	pound pancetta (Italian cured bacon) or lean bacon, diced		1	cup half-and-half
1	small onion, finely diced		1/2	teaspoon salt
1	teaspoon minced garlic		1/4	teaspoon ground black pepper
4	large eggs		1	cup grated Romano cheese
				additional freshly ground pepper
			1/4	cup chopped fresh parsley

Have the cooked pasta warmed and ready to use in the sauce. In a large skillet, sauté the pancetta or bacon and onion for 5 minutes on low heat until bacon is crisp and onion is browned. Add the minced garlic and the cooked pasta to the pan and toss well to coat, cooking about 2 minutes on medium heat. Pasta should be heated through. While pasta is heating, make the sauce quickly.

In large mixing bowl, beat the eggs, egg yolks, half-and-half, salt, pepper and grated cheese. Toss the hot pasta with onion and pancetta in the bowl with egg mixture. Toss quickly until well combined. The heat of the pasta should "cook" the eggs slightly. Add a little more coarsely ground black pepper and chopped parsley. Serve immediately.

Serves 4 to 6

Note: This is a dish that waits for no one. Have your guests ready to eat as soon as the pasta is added to the egg mixture.

This is my son Justin's favorite pasta dish. When he was in the 4th grade he was asked to fill out a questionnaire by his teacher on the first day of school of the favorite foods of the students. When other children answered "pizza," "hot dogs," or "French fries," Justin wrote "Spaghetti alla Carbonara." When asked by his teacher what it was, he said it was bacon and eggs with pasta and that his mom would come to class some day and make it for all the 25 students in his class. And his mom did. And they loved it, too.

Penne Pasta with Pancetta Tomato Sauce

1/4 pound diced pancetta or bacon
2 tablespoons olive oil
1 large onion, diced
  28-ounce can crushed Italian
  tomatoes with juices
1/2 cup sun-dried tomatoes
1 cup dry red wine or beef broth
1 teaspoon salt

1/2 teaspoon ground black pepper
1 teaspoon dried oregano
1 pound imported penne pasta
1 cup ricotta
1/2 cup chopped fresh parsley
1/2 cup grated Romano or Parmesan
  cheese

In large skillet, sauté the pancetta or bacon, oil and onion on low heat until pancetta is golden brown, about 10 minutes. Add the canned tomatoes, sun-dried tomatoes, wine, salt, pepper and oregano. Cover; simmer for 20 minutes. While sauce is cooking, boil pasta until done, drain and add to sauce, tossing to coat evenly. Serve at once with dollops of ricotta on top and chopped parsley. Pass the grated cheese separately.

Serves 4

Rigatoni with a Creamy Fontina-Sausage Sauce

1 pound imported rigatoni pasta,
  cooked slightly underdone, drained
2 tablespoons olive oil
1 pound bulk sweet Italian sausage
1 tablespoon minced garlic
  pinch of red pepper flakes
1/2 teaspoon fennel seeds
1 tablespoon dried oregano

1 tablespoon dried basil
  28-ounce can crushed Italian
  tomatoes with juices
1/2 teaspoon salt
1/2 cup heavy cream
1/2 pound fontina cheese, cut into
  small dice
1/2 cup grated Romano cheese

Place pasta in a 9×13-inch baking dish. Set aside. In a large skillet, heat oil. Sauté the sausage for 5 minutes, crumbling as you cook. Add the garlic, red pepper flakes, fennel seeds, oregano and basil. Sauté for another minute. Add tomatoes, salt and cream. Cover and simmer for 10 minutes. Add the sauce to the pasta, sprinkle with fontina and Romano cheeses. Cover loosely with foil. Bake in a preheated 375-degree oven for 20 minutes. Serve at once.

Serves 4 to 6

Herb-Roasted Leg of Lamb

	5- to 6-pound leg of lamb, boned and butterflied (have butcher do this for you)	1	teaspoon kosher salt
		1/4	teaspoon ground black pepper
		1/4	cup olive oil
2	tablespoons minced garlic	1	lemon, thinly sliced
1/4	cup chopped fresh rosemary leaves	2	large onions, thinly sliced
2	tablespoons chopped fresh oregano	2	cups red wine or beef broth

Lay the lamb flat on work surface, fat side down. In a small bowl, combine the garlic, rosemary, oregano, salt, pepper and oil. Rub the lamb with herb mixture, reserving a tablespoon or two for top. Place the sliced lemon on the herbs and roll up the lamb "jelly roll" style and tie with kitchen string at 1-inch intervals. Rub the outside of the lamb with remaining herb mixture. Place lamb roast in a roasting pan (on a rack, if desired). Place sliced onions around the lamb. Roast in a preheated 400-degree oven for 10 minutes; reduce heat to 325 degrees and roast for an additional 15 minutes per pound. After 1 hour, add 1 cup red wine or beef broth to pan and continue to roast until internal temperature reaches 140 degrees for medium doneness. Remove the roast to a serving platter and allow to "rest" before slicing into thin pieces. Deglaze the pan with the remaining 1 cup red wine or beef broth and serve the lamb with roasted onions and pan juices.

Serves 6 to 8

Note: This is the perfect dish for Easter Sunday dinner or a spring dinner party. It epitomizes all the flavors of a good lamb with the onions, garlic, herbs and wine. It can be stuffed and rolled the day before roasting and then refrigerated until ready to use. This allows all the flavors to be enhanced through the lamb.

Lamb Burgers with Yogurt Dill Sauce

2   pounds ground lamb
1   tablespoon minced garlic
1   teaspoon salt
1/4 teaspoon ground black pepper
1/2 cup minced onion

1/4 cup chopped fresh mint leaves or
     1 tablespoon dried mint leaves
2   tablespoons chopped fresh oregano
     leaves or 2 teaspoons dried oregano
1   large egg

In medium bowl, combine all ingredients for burgers. Mix well and form into 8 burgers, 1/2 inch thick and 3 inches in diameter. Heat grill to medium or add 1 tablespoon olive oil to a 10-inch skillet on medium heat. Grill burgers for 4 to 5 minutes per side, or fry in the olive oil in the skillet, 4 to 5 minutes per side. Burgers should be slightly pink in the center.

To make sandwiches

4   pita bread rounds, cut in half to
     form "pockets"
2   large tomatoes, coarsely chopped

1   onion, thinly sliced
1   green pepper, thinly sliced

Place one burger in one half of sliced pita bread. Tuck in some tomatoes, onion, green pepper and top with 2 tablespoons Yogurt Dill Sauce. Serve at once.

Makes 8 sandwiches

Yogurt Dill Sauce

8   ounces (1 cup) container plain
     yogurt
1   tablespoon dried dillweed
1   tablespoon sugar
1/2 teaspoon salt

1/4 teaspoon ground white pepper
2   tablespoons finely chopped onion
2   tablespoons chopped fresh mint or
     2 teaspoons dried mint leaves

Combine all ingredients in small bowl 1 hour before serving. Cover with plastic wrap and refrigerate until ready to use.

Makes about 1 1/2 cups sauce

Oven-Roasted Mediterranean Chicken

	3- to 4-pound whole roasting chicken, cleaned and patted dry
1	whole onion
1	carrot, halved
1	lemon, halved
2	sprigs fresh rosemary
6	to 8 whole cloves garlic, peeled kosher salt and pepper
2	pounds new potatoes, cut into 1-inch dice
1	cup pitted kalamata olives
1	large onion, peeled and diced
1	pound mushrooms, sliced
1	bulb fresh fennel, sliced (save fronds for garnish)
4	tablespoons olive oil
1	cup white wine, chicken broth or water

Place cleaned chicken in roasting pan. Place whole onion with skin on, carrot halves and lemon halves in cavity of chicken. Place rosemary under skin of chicken, garlic cloves around chicken, and season the top and inside cavity of chicken with kosher salt and pepper. Roast in 450-degree oven for 20 minutes. Reduce heat to 375 degrees and add potatoes, olives, onion, mushrooms and fennel. Drizzle with olive oil. Continue to roast for an additional 45 minutes to 1 hour, depending on size of chicken, stirring vegetables often. Remove pan from oven; test chicken for doneness. Remove chicken and vegetables from pan. Allow chicken to "rest" 5 minutes before carving. Add the wine, broth or water to roasting pan; deglaze over burner by stirring liquid in pan for 1 minute over medium heat. Serve pan drippings over chicken with vegetables on side. Chop the fronds from fennel and sprinkle on top.

Serves 4

Oven-Roasted Ten-Herb Chicken in Pan Juices with Potatoes and Green Beans

1/2 cup olive oil
5 cloves garlic, thinly sliced
1 tablespoon of each: basil, tarragon, chives, oregano, thyme, parsley, marjoram, sage, rosemary and mint—all finely chopped

1 tablespoon kosher salt
1/2 teaspoon black pepper
4 chicken halves (about 1 1/2 pounds each)

Combine all the ingredients except chicken halves in a large bowl. Toss chicken in marinade and coat well with all the fresh herbs. Allow to marinate in refrigerator at least 2 hours and up to 8 hours. Remove to a baking pan, skin side up, and roast in a 500-degree oven for 10 minutes. Reduce the heat to 325 degrees and roast until chicken is golden and tender, about 45 more minutes. Remove pan from oven, transfer chicken halves to a warmed plate and add 1 cup water to pan to deglaze over low heat on burner. Using a wooden spoon, scrape bits from bottom of pan. Serve with Potatoes and Green Beans and pan juices over the chicken halves.

Serves 4

Potatoes and Green Beans

2 pounds small white new potatoes or fingerling potatoes, cooked until tender
1 pound fresh green beans, cleaned
1 tablespoon salt

4 tablespoons olive oil
1 clove garlic, minced
2 tablespoons chopped fresh parsley
1/2 teaspoon salt
1/4 teaspoon ground black pepper

Cut the cooked potatoes into 1-inch dice. Blanch green beans in 2 cups boiling water mixed with the 1 tablespoon salt and 2 tablespoons of the olive oil for 3 minutes. Drain. In a medium bowl, combine the potatoes, beans, remaining olive oil, garlic, parsley and 1/2 teaspoon salt and pepper. Serve warm alongside the chicken.

Note: This is a flavorful way of utilizing the herbs in your garden. If all these fresh herbs are not available, then use as many as you can find. All these herbs go well with poultry.

Chicken alla Cucina

2	tablespoons butter		2	cups chicken broth
1	tablespoon olive oil		1	cup dry white wine
1	medium onion, diced		1/2	cup julienne-cut sun-dried tomatoes
1	tablespoon chopped garlic		1	teaspoon dried oregano
1 1/2	pounds boneless and skinless chicken breasts, cut into 1-inch pieces		1	teaspoon dried basil
2	tablespoons flour		1	teaspoon salt
	15-ounce can artichoke hearts, drained and coarsely chopped		1/2	teaspoon ground black pepper

In a large skillet, heat the butter and olive oil. Add the onion; sauté for at least 2 to 3 minutes or until softened. Add garlic and chicken pieces. Sauté until chicken is cooked through. Stir in the flour until incorporated in the chicken pieces. Add artichokes, chicken broth, white wine, sun-dried tomatoes, oregano, basil, salt and pepper. Cover; simmer for 10 minutes, stirring often. Taste for seasoning. Serve over steamed rice, polenta or orzo pasta.

Serves 4 to 6

Note: We have made hundreds of pounds of Chicken alla Cucina for our customers, whether for catering orders, luncheons or the deli case. It remains a staple and one of the best sellers in the restaurant.

Chicken Vegetable Pot Pie with Parmesan Crust

Filling

2	pounds boneless, skinless chicken breasts	2	cups diced white new potatoes
2	bay leaves	1/2	pound button mushrooms, sliced
1	teaspoon salt	1	teaspoon dried thyme
1/4	teaspoon ground black pepper	1	teaspoon salt
4	tablespoons butter	1/2	teaspoon white pepper
1	leek, white part only, thinly sliced	4	ounces butter (1 stick)
4	ribs celery, thinly sliced	1/2	cup flour
2	carrots, peeled and thinly sliced	1	cup half-and-half
1	cup frozen petite peas	1	cup chicken broth (from poaching liquid)

Poach chicken for 20 minutes in 4 cups simmering water with bay leaves, salt and pepper. Remove chicken; reserve broth. Cut chicken into 1-inch cubes. In a saucepan, heat butter and sauté the leek, celery, carrots, peas, potatoes, mushrooms, thyme and salt and pepper for 2 minutes or until softened. Add to bowl with chicken. In same saucepan, heat remaining butter over medium heat and whisk in the flour to make a "roux." Add half-and-half and 1 cup reserved broth. Whisk until smooth, about 3 minutes. Taste for seasoning. Add to vegetable mixture and toss well.

Crust

2 1/2	cups flour	1	teaspoon salt
4	tablespoons butter		pinch of cayenne pepper
4	tablespoons shortening	8	tablespoons iced water
1/2	cup grated Parmesan cheese		Egg wash: 1 egg beaten with 1
2	tablespoons chopped fresh parsley		tablespoon cream
1	teaspoon dried thyme		

In bowl of food processor, combine the flour, butter and shortening. Pulse on and off until dough is the size of peas. Add the cheese, parsley, thyme, salt and cayenne pepper. Pulse again until combined, about 5 pulses. With motor running slowly pour in the water until dough forms a ball, about 30 seconds. Remove to floured board and roll to a 12-inch diameter.

Place the pot pie filling in a 4-quart ovenproof pan. Top with dough, making sure dough covers filling. Crimp edges. Brush with an egg wash. Bake at 375 degrees for 30 minutes or until crust is golden and filling is bubbly. Remove from oven and serve at once.

Serves 6 to 8

Chicken and Seafood Paella

1/4	cup olive oil		1/2	teaspoon black pepper
8	chicken legs		1/2	teaspoon saffron threads
8	chicken thighs		1	cup white wine
	salt and pepper		2	pounds (about 24) mussels
3	tablespoons chopped fresh garlic		2	pounds (about 24) clams
1/4	cup olive oil		2	pounds large raw shrimp, peeled
1	large onion, peeled and thinly sliced			and deveined
1	red pepper, sliced julienne			15-ounce can artichoke hearts,
1	green pepper, sliced julienne			drained
2	cups converted rice		2	cups frozen petite peas, thawed
4	cups chicken broth		1	cup chopped fresh parsley
1/2	teaspoon salt		2	limes, thinly sliced

In a large sauté pan, heat oil over medium heat. Sprinkle chicken pieces with a little salt and pepper and add to skillet, skin side down, and cook chicken until golden brown. You may have to do this in batches, eight pieces at a time. Turn over chicken pieces, add 1 tablespoon garlic to pan and brown other side of chicken. Sauté the chicken until it is completely cooked through. Remove to a platter. Deglaze the pan with 1 cup water and reserve that liquid. (This process may be done a day ahead, then refrigerate chicken and reserved liquid until ready to make paella.)

To Make Paella: In a large paella pan or 14-inch deep skillet, heat oil over medium heat. Add onion, peppers and remaining 2 tablespoons garlic and cook until softened, about 2 minutes, stirring often. Add the rice, chicken broth mixed with the salt, pepper and saffron threads, reserved chicken liquid and wine. Cook on low heat, stirring often until most of the liquid is absorbed. This should take about 20 minutes. Add the chicken pieces in decorative manner by pressing the chicken into the rice, place mussels and clams on and around the rice, with pointed sides of the mollusks down, place shrimp on top, add artichokes and peas and cover pan with foil or large cover so that seafood can "steam" in the mixture. Cook the rice on medium heat for 15 minutes or until clams and mussels have opened and the shrimp are pink. This may take up to 20 minutes, depending on the size of the clams and mussels used. Discard any unopened clams or mussels at this point. Sprinkle the paella with chopped parsley and place lime slices around the perimeter of paella. Serve at once.

Serves 8 to 12

Note: This is a great summertime dinner on the patio. It serves a group, can
be done on the grill over low heat and is an impressive dish to serve to a crowd. I have
done this many times for summer patio parties, serving Sangria and Margaritas
along with imported beers as beverages and Orange Flan (page 122) for dessert.

Herb-Roasted Turkey Breast with Dried Fruit Dressing

1	whole turkey breast, about 8 pounds	8	cups fresh bread crumbs	
1/2	cup chopped fresh mixed herbs (use a combination of any of the following: basil, parsley, thyme, sage, mint, rosemary, chives, etc.)	1	large onion, diced	
		1	tablespoon herbes de Provence or 1 tablespoon dried thyme	
1/4	cup melted butter	1	cup diced dried mixed fruits	
1/2	teaspoon salt	1/2	to 1 cup half-and-half	
1/2	teaspoon black pepper	1	teaspoon salt	
		1/2	teaspoon ground black pepper	

Place turkey on work surface. With a sharp knife, split the turkey backbone in half to flatten the breast. Combine herbs, butter, salt and pepper in small bowl. Rub the entire surface (skin side) with herb mixture, spreading some under skin, too. Set turkey aside. In mixing bowl, combine bread crumbs, onion, dried herbs, mixed fruits and enough half-and-half to moisten bread. Add salt and pepper. Place fruit dressing in the center of a baking dish large enough to hold the turkey. Place the turkey on top of stuffing. Place in 350-degree oven and roast for 1 1/2 hours. Test with meat thermometer. Center of turkey should read 180 degrees. Remove turkey from pan. Allow to "rest" 5 minutes before slicing. Slice breast into thin pieces, top with dressing and serve.

Serves 8 to 10

Grilled Honey Mustard Game Hens

1/4	cup honey		juice of 1 lemon	
1/4	cup molasses	1	teaspoon ground dry mustard	
3/4	cup apricot preserves	4	Cornish game hens, split in half through breastbone or 4 chicken halves (2 whole chickens, cut in half)	
2	tablespoons soy sauce			
1	teaspoon freshly grated ginger			
1	teaspoon lemon zest			

In a small saucepan, combine honey, molasses, apricot preserves, soy sauce, ginger, lemon zest, lemon juice and dry mustard. Simmer on low heat for 5 minutes. Heat grill to medium. Place game hens or chicken skin side down on grill; lower heat to low. Brush with sauce. Cook for 15 minutes. Turn game hens or chickens and baste with remaining sauce. Grill for an additional 15 to 20 minutes.

Serves 4

Note: Use this sauce on pork chops, pork tenderloins, lamb chops or salmon fillets.

Almond-Crusted Salmon Fillets with Zucchini and Carrots Julienne

2   eggs, beaten
1   cup coarsely ground almonds
1/2   cup flour
1/2   teaspoon salt
1/4   teaspoon ground black pepper
4   (8-ounce) skinless salmon fillets
2   tablespoons butter
2   carrots, thinly sliced or cut julienne on a mandoline
2   zucchini, thinly sliced or cut julienne on a mandoline

1/2   teaspoon salt
1/4   teaspoon ground black pepper
1/2   cup half-and-half
1   tablespoon chopped fresh tarragon or 1 teaspoon dried tarragon
3   to 4 cups cooked white and wild rice mixture, couscous or mashed potatoes

Garnish

4   sprigs fresh tarragon, parsley or thyme

Place beaten eggs in shallow pan. Place almonds, flour, salt and pepper on waxed paper or shallow pan. Dip salmon fillets in eggs then in almond mixture, coating well on both sides. Place on greased baking pan.

Bake in preheated 375-degree oven for 8 to 10 minutes, depending on thickness of salmon fillets. While salmon is cooking, heat butter in medium skillet. Sauté the carrots and zucchini with the salt and pepper for 2 minutes on medium heat, or until cooked but still crispy. Add half-and-half and tarragon. Cook another minute, stirring while cooking. Remove from heat.

Place a serving of rice, couscous or potatoes in center of each plate. Top with a salmon fillet, then with 1/4 of the zucchini and carrot sauté with some of the sauce. Serve at once with a sprig of tarragon on top.

Serves 4

Note: This is an easy and lower in fat method of obtaining a crispy crust on outside of fish, such as salmon, without the mess of frying. The tarragon is a wonderful complement to the salmon, also. It is a complete meal with the addition of the rice, couscous or potatoes.

Salmon en Croûte

*This is a wonderful dish for the large dinner party or buffet when you want
to really impress your guests.*

2	packages (17 ounces each) storebought puff pastry sheets, thawed in refrigerator	4	Roma tomatoes, coarsely chopped
1	whole skinless salmon side (about 4 pounds)	2	teaspoons dried thyme
2	ounces (1/2 stick) butter	1/2	teaspoon salt
2	leeks, white part only, cleaned and thinly sliced	1/4	teaspoon ground black pepper

1/2 teaspoon salt

1/4 teaspoon ground black pepper

Egg Wash: 1 large egg beaten with
1 tablespoon half-and-half

Place puff pastry on work surface. Roll the 4 pieces together to form one large sheet. (Two sheets are on top, two on bottom to form one large square.) Place salmon on upper half of pastry. In a medium sauté pan, heat butter and sauté the leeks until soft, about 5 minutes. Add tomatoes, thyme, salt and pepper. Sauté another 2 minutes. Cool to room temperature. Place the leek mixture evenly on the salmon fillet. Roll bottom half of pastry over the salmon (like an envelope) and secure the edges by crimping close to the salmon in a decorative manner. Cut away any excess pastry. Carefully lift the salmon to a parchment-lined baking sheet. Use any excess pastry for garnishing the salmon with pastry cutouts of "leaves," "roses" or a lattice across the top of the salmon. Brush with egg wash. Score the top of pastry lightly with crisscross lines 2 inches apart and bake in 425-degree oven for 20 to 25 minutes or until golden brown. Remove; cool for 10 minutes before transferring to a serving platter and cut into 2-inch wide slices. Serve with Cucumber Dill Sauce if desired or just as is.

Serves 8 as part of a buffet

Cucumber Dill Sauce

1	cup (8 ounces) sour cream	1	teaspoon sugar
1/2	cup mayonnaise	1	teaspoon dried dillweed or 1 tablespoon chopped fresh dill
1	large cucumber, peeled and seeded, coarsely chopped	1/2	teaspoon salt
2	tablespoons chopped onion	1/4	teaspoon white pepper

Place all ingredients in a blender or food processor and process until smooth, about 30 seconds. Taste for seasoning. Refrigerate until ready to use.

Makes about 1 1/2 cups sauce

Salmon Spirals with Red Pepper Pesto

4-pound side of skinless salmon
8 (6-inch) wooden skewers
2 cups water seasoned with 2 bay leaves, 1 teaspoon peppercorns, 1/2 teaspoon salt

4 cups mixed greens
2 lemons, thinly sliced

Place salmon side on work surface. Trim off excess fat. With a sharp knife, cut lengthwise down the salmon to form 8 strips about 3/4 inch wide × 12 inches long. Roll each strip into a spiral and secure with wooden skewer. Place in baking dish or pan with seasoned water; cover with foil and bake in 375-degree oven for 10 minutes or until opaque. Cool salmon for 5 minutes in water; with a spatula, carefully remove to a plate and chill for 1 hour before serving on a platter lined with fresh mixed greens and lemon slices around perimeter of platter.

Red Pepper Pesto

1 cup roasted red pepper pieces (or 2 red peppers, roasted in oven, skins removed)
1/2 teaspoon salt

1/4 teaspoon ground black pepper
1/2 cup chopped fresh basil leaves
1 tablespoon minced garlic
1/3 cup olive oil

In a food processor, purée the roasted peppers. Add the salt, pepper, basil and garlic. Slowly add the oil until all ingredients are incorporated.

Garnish

8 sprigs fresh basil leaves

1/4 cup diced red bell pepper

Drizzle pesto over salmon; decorate with fresh basil leaves and finely diced red peppers.

Serves 8

Note: Use green and red pesto sauces during holidays. In the summer months, try this dish with Cucumber Dill Sauce (page 101) placed in dollops on each salmon spiral.

Salmon in Parchment

4	(14×14-inch) pieces parchment paper	1	leek, white part only, cut julienne
4	(8-ounce) salmon fillets	1	teaspoon dried thyme
1	carrot, peeled and cut julienne	1/2	teaspoon salt
1	zucchini, cut julienne	1/4	teaspoon ground black pepper
		4	tablespoons butter

Place parchment paper on work surface. Place one salmon fillet in center of each parchment paper. Place the carrots, zucchini, leek, thyme, salt and pepper in a small bowl. Place 1/4 of the vegetable mixture on top of salmon, top each with 1 tablespoon of butter and fold over the parchment to form a triangle, with ends of paper even. Fold the ends of parchment over so that the paper is secure and there are no air pockets in each packet. Continue with remaining salmon and vegetables. Place on a baking sheet. (Can be made ahead up to this point and then refrigerated.) Bake in preheated 375-degree oven for 10 minutes. Remove from oven and serve each packet cut with an X on top to allow steam to escape.

Serves 4

Mussels Marinara

3	to 4 pounds mussels, debearded and washed	1	teaspoon dried basil
2	tablespoons olive oil		28-ounce can chopped Italian tomatoes with juices
2	tablespoons butter	1	cup dry white wine
1/2	cup diced onion	1/2	teaspoon salt
2	tablespoons minced garlic	1/4	teaspoon ground black pepper
1	teaspoon dried oregano		Optional: 2 anchovy fillets, diced

Garnish

1/4 cup chopped fresh parsley

Have the mussels cleaned and iced in large bowl. In large stockpot, heat oil and butter. Sauté the onion until soft, about 3 minutes on medium heat. Add garlic, oregano and basil. Sauté 1 minute. Add tomatoes, wine, salt and pepper. If you are adding anchovies, do so now. Cover pot; simmer for 15 minutes. (Can be done up to 1 day ahead, then reheated when ready to add mussels.) While sauce is simmering, add mussels; cover and cook over medium-high heat for 5 to 8 minutes, stirring occasionally. When mussels have opened, serve in large bowls, topped with parsley, and with crusty bread to soak up the juices.

Serves 4 to 6

Mussels in Pernod Cream Sauce over Linguine

4	tablespoons butter		2	tablespoons Pernod, sambuca or ouzo
2	shallots, peeled and minced		1	cup half-and-half
1/4	teaspoon white pepper		1	pound imported linguine, cooked "al dente," drained
1/2	cup chopped fresh parsley			
1/2	cup dry white wine		1/4	cup chopped fresh parsley
3	pounds fresh mussels, cleaned			

In a large saucepan, heat butter and sauté the shallots for 3 minutes or until soft and translucent. Add the white pepper, parsley, wine and mussels. Cover; cook on medium-high heat until mussels have opened. Add Pernod and cream. Simmer for another minute. Place pasta in a large serving bowl. Pour mussels and sauce over pasta and serve with chopped fresh parsley on top.

Serves 4

Fettuccine with Creamy Champagne Shrimp Sauce

1	pound imported fettuccine pasta, cooked "al dente," drained		1/4	teaspoon salt
2	tablespoons butter		1	cup heavy cream
2	shallots, peeled and chopped		1	cup sparkling white wine or champagne
1/4	teaspoon red pepper flakes			
1	tablespoon minced garlic		1	pound large (21 to 25 per pound) raw shrimp, peeled and deveined
4	large Roma tomatoes, chopped			
2	tablespoons chopped fresh basil		1/4	cup chopped fresh parsley

While pasta is cooking, make the sauce. In a large skillet, heat butter and sauté the shallots until soft, about 2 minutes over medium heat. Add the red pepper flakes and garlic. Sauté another minute; add the Roma tomatoes, basil, salt, cream and wine. Simmer for 2 minutes. Add shrimp, cook for another 3 to 4 minutes or until shrimp turn pink. Stir in the parsley. Pour the sauce over cooked pasta and serve at once.

Serves 4

Jumbo Shrimp Parmigiana

2   pounds raw shrimp (11 to 15 per pound), peeled and deveined (if jumbo aren't available, use the largest shrimp you can find)
2   cups flour
3   eggs, beaten
2   cups seasoned bread crumbs

$1/2$ cup vegetable or canola oil
2   cups Basic Tomato Sauce (page 84)
$1/2$ pound shredded mozzarella
$1/2$ cup grated Romano cheese
1   tablespoon dried oregano
$1/4$ cup chopped fresh parsley

Clean shrimp; pat dry. Dredge shrimp in flour, then dip in beaten eggs and then in seasoned bread crumbs. Shake off excess crumbs. When all the shrimp are breaded, heat oil in a large skillet. Fry shrimp, 4 or 5 at a time, until golden brown (it is not necessary to cook through, since they will be baked further); remove to a baking pan in a single layer. Top with tomato sauce, mozzarella, Romano cheese and dried oregano. Bake, uncovered, in a preheated 400-degree oven for 10 minutes or until cheese is melted. Top with chopped fresh parsley.

Serves 8 (allows 3 or 4 shrimp per person)

Note: I remember this dish served as a course at our Sunday dinners, on Friday nights when it was meatless Fridays and at family parties as part of a buffet. It evokes warm memories of delicious aromas of cheese, shrimp and sauce.

Linguine with Seafood
(Linguine alla Tutto Mare)

1	pound imported linguine pasta	1	teaspoon salt
1	tablespoon olive oil	1/4	teaspoon ground black pepper
1/4	cup olive oil	2	pounds fresh mussels, cleaned and debearded
1	medium onion, diced		
2	tablespoons minced garlic	1	pound cockles, manila or other small clam
	pinch of red pepper flakes		
	28-ounce can diced Italian plum tomatoes with their juices	1	pound raw large shrimp (21 to 26 per pound), peeled and deveined
1	cup dry white wine	1	pound calamari (squid), cleaned and cut into rings
1	teaspoon dried oregano		
1	tablespoon sugar		

Garnish

1/4 cup chopped fresh basil

Cook pasta; set aside in a bowl tossed with 1 tablespoon olive oil and keep warm. In large saucepan, heat 1/4 cup olive oil over medium heat. Add onion and sauté until soft. Add garlic and red pepper flakes. Cook 1 minute on low heat. Add the tomatoes, wine, oregano, sugar, salt and pepper. Cover; simmer for 10 minutes. (The sauce can be made ahead up to this point.) Add the mussels and clams and cover; cook over medium heat for 5 to 8 minutes until mussels and clams open. Add the shrimp and calamari. Cook for 2 or 3 minutes until shrimp are pink. Do not overcook the shrimp and calamari. Discard any unopened mussels or clams at this point. Place warm pasta in serving dish, top with seafood sauce and serve at once with chopped fresh basil on top.

Serves 4 to 6

Note: This is such a popular dish in restaurants and yet so easy to make at home. My family loves this dish, with crusty bread and a large green salad. You can easily change the seafood as you desire, doubling the shrimp or clams, as desired. Just remember not to overcook the seafood.

Manicotti (Cheese-Filled Crepes)

Batter for Crepes (The Pasta)

1	cup cold water	1/2	teaspoon salt
1	cup cold milk	2	cups flour
4	large eggs	4	tablespoons melted butter

In blender or with a whisk, blend ingredients until smooth and there are no lumps. Cover; refrigerate 1 hour. Heat a nonstick 6-inch crepe pan or omelette pan over medium-high heat. Rub with a little butter or spray with nonstick vegetable spray. Add 2 tablespoons batter to pan, tilting to spread batter evenly. Cook on medium-high heat for 30 seconds until no longer runny, carefully lift, turn and cook an additional 10 seconds. Remove to plate. Continue using remaining batter, cooking for just about 40 seconds per crepe. Add more butter to pan or spray pan after fourth or fifth crepe.

Makes about 16 crepes

Filling

2	pounds whole milk ricotta	2	eggs
1	pound fresh mozzarella, cubed or shredded	1/2	teaspoon salt
1	cup grated Parmesan or Romano cheese	1/4	teaspoon ground black pepper

Topping

3	to 4 cups tomato sauce	1/4	cup grated Parmesan or Romano cheese

Mix all filling ingredients in a bowl until well combined. Place a crepe on work surface and spoon about 2 tablespoons filling in center. Roll up crepe and place in a baking dish in a single layer, seam side down, with a thin layer of tomato sauce on bottom. Continue using crepes and filling until all used (makes about 16 manicotti). Top the manicotti with tomato sauce of your choice. Sprinkle with grated cheese and bake, covered with foil, for 30 minutes in 350-degree oven until bubbly and cheeses have melted. Serve immediately. (Can be made hours ahead, refrigerated, then baked.)

Makes about 16 manicotti

Pasta with Ricotta

1/2 pound imported ancini de pepe,
   orzo, ditali or ditalini pasta
1 teaspoon salt
2 quarts water
1/2 pound whole milk ricotta

ground black pepper
3 to 4 tablespoons extra-virgin
   olive oil
2 to 3 tablespoons grated Parmesan
   cheese

In 2 quarts of salted water, boil pasta until "al dente" in a medium saucepan. Drain off some of the water, leaving 1 inch of the water in the saucepan with the pasta. Place the saucepan back on low heat, add the ricotta, black pepper to taste and olive oil. Cook for only 1 minute on low heat, just until ricotta is heated through. Ladle into soup bowls; top with grated cheese and a little more black pepper. Serve at once.

Serves 2 or 3

Spaghetti alla Margherita

1 pound imported spaghetti, cooked
   "al dente," drained
1/4 cup olive oil
2 tablespoons butter
2 large cloves garlic, slivered
10 large Roma tomatoes (about 2
   pounds), coarsely chopped
1 teaspoon sugar

1 teaspoon salt
1/2 teaspoon ground black pepper
1 cup fresh basil leaves, coarsely
   chopped
1/2 pound fresh mozzarella, cut into
   1/2-inch cubes
1/2 cup freshly grated Romano pecorino
   cheese

Cook spaghetti while making the sauce. In large skillet, heat olive oil and butter over low heat. Add the slivered garlic and cook for 30 seconds or until fragrant. Add the chopped tomatoes, sugar, salt and pepper. Cover; simmer for 10 minutes. Add the chopped fresh basil and the cooked spaghetti. Cook for 2 or 3 minutes on low heat to warm the pasta thoroughly. Remove pan from heat, place steaming hot pasta and sauce in a large serving bowl, toss in the fresh mozzarella and grated cheese. Stir well and serve at once.

Serves 4

This is my friend and business partner Eileen's favorite dish. It was required fare when we were discussing Cucina's finances in our lean years, entertaining our valued clients or just in the mood for comfort food on those very bad days when pasta and a glass of chianti are your only friends. It is simple, sensuous and satiating!

Penne alla Vodka

1	pound imported penne pasta, cooked "al dente," drained		pinch of red pepper flakes	
1/2	stick (2 ounces) butter	2	cups puréed canned Italian tomatoes	
1/4	cup chopped onion	2	cups chicken broth	
2	cloves garlic, slivered	2	cups half-and-half	
8	ounces fresh mushrooms, thinly sliced	1/4	cup vodka	
		1	teaspoon salt	
1	teaspoon dried thyme	1/4	teaspoon ground black pepper	
		1/4	cup grated Romano cheese	

Cook the pasta while making the sauce. It will take as long to make the sauce as to cook the pasta "al dente," about 8 minutes.

In a large skillet, heat butter. Add onion and cook for 2 minutes on medium heat or until soft. Add garlic, mushrooms, thyme and red pepper flakes. Sauté for another minute or until the mushrooms are slightly softened. Add the tomatoes, broth and half-and-half. Simmer on low heat for 3 to 4 minutes. (Can be made ahead up to this point.) Add vodka, salt and pepper and taste for seasoning. Cook another 2 minutes on medium heat. Place penne in a large serving bowl, top with sauce and sprinkle with grated Romano cheese.

Serves 4

Note: This is a popular dish found in most Italian restaurants back East. I love this pasta because it is easy, flavorful and ingredients are easily available all year round. The alcohol will cook out, so have no fears of feeding this to underage diners.

New York-Style Pizza

Classic Pizza Dough

1	teaspoon active dry yeast	1	teaspoon salt
2/3	cup warm water (110 degrees)	2	tablespoons olive oil
2	cups all-purpose flour		oil for bowl

Sprinkle yeast over water and let stand 1 minute. Stir until yeast dissolves. In bowl, combine the flour, salt and olive oil. Stir in the water and yeast. Stir until soft dough forms. Knead for 5 minutes, adding more flour if dough is wet. Coat a bowl with oil. Add dough; wrap in plastic; allow to rise 1 1/2 hours. Flatten dough on work surface. Roll out to a 12-inch diameter. Place on pizza stone or on round pizza tray.

Topping

2	cups Basic Tomato Sauce (page 84)	1	tablespoon dried oregano
1	pound fresh mozzarella, thinly sliced	1	teaspoon red pepper flakes
1/2	cup grated Romano cheese	2	tablespoons olive oil
1/4	cup chopped fresh basil		

Spread sauce evenly over dough to 1/2 inch of edge of dough. Sprinkle on mozzarella, grated cheese, basil, oregano and red pepper flakes. Drizzle pizza with the olive oil. Bake on bottom shelf of 475-degree oven for 12 to 15 minutes or until crispy and cheese is bubbly. Serve at once.

Serves 2 to 4

Desserts

*Savor the Memories of my mother's Blue Doulton...
little china cups of espresso with lemon zest and
crystal bowls of oven-roasted whole nuts ready to be
cracked after dinner on Sundays and holidays.*

Almond-Stuffed Pears in Puff Pastry with "Faux Crème Anglaise"

1	package (17 ounces), store-bought frozen puff pastry, thawed	1	tablespoon sugar
2	large Comice or D'Anjou pears, peeled	2	tablespoons butter
	juice of 1 lemon	1/2	teaspoon almond extract
1/2	cup whole almonds		zest of 1 lemon
			egg wash: 1 egg beaten with 1 tablespoon half-and-half

Place the 2 sheets of puff pastry on work surface. Cut each piece in half to have 4 sheets of pastry. Cut each pear in half, lengthwise. Core with melon baller. Place pear halves in a bowl with 2 cups water and juice of 1 lemon while making almond paste. In food processor, grind almonds with sugar, butter, almond extract and lemon zest until it forms a thick paste. Press 1 tablespoon filling into the center of each pear. Place each pear half, flat side up, on each cut piece of pastry. Fold pastry over pear, sealing the pastry and cutting away the excess pastry. Turn pear over and place on parchment paper-lined baking sheet, round side up, and brush with the egg wash. Use the extra puff pastry pieces to cut out "leaves" for the pears and attach to top of each. Bake in a 400-degree oven for 20 minutes. Remove from oven. Serve warm with "Faux Crème Anglaise."

Makes 4 servings

"Faux Crème Anglaise"

2	cups Canadian vanilla ice cream	1/2	teaspoon vanilla extract

Melt ice cream to room temperature and stir in vanilla extract. Pour about 1/2 cup melted ice cream on a serving plate, top with a warmed pear half and serve with a mint sprig.

Grilled Bananas and Pineapple in Brown Sugar Rum Sauce on Vanilla Ice Cream

2   under-ripe bananas, peeled and cut in half lengthwise, then crosswise (8 pieces)

2   tablespoons melted butter

1   pineapple, peeled, cored and cut into eight 1-inch wide wedges (reserve extra for another use)

4   scoops vanilla ice cream

Grill bananas on both sides over medium heat, brushing with some of the melted butter until golden. Grill pineapple slices on both sides, brushing with remaining butter until golden.

Place one scoop ice cream in serving bowl. Place 2 pieces banana and 2 pieces pineapple on each ice cream scoop and top with 2 tablespoons rum sauce. Garnish with fresh mint leaves.

Serves 4

Brown Sugar Rum Sauce

4   tablespoons butter

1   cup brown sugar

1/2   teaspoon cinnamon

zest and juice of 1 orange

1/4   cup dark rum

In a small saucepan, combine all ingredients; cook on low heat until sugar is melted. (Can be made one day ahead, then reheated before serving.)

Makes about 1 cup sauce

Panettone Bread Pudding with Rum Sauce

10	eggs		2	cups fresh cranberries
1	quart half-and-half		1	cup pecan pieces
1/2	cup sugar			zest and juice of 1 orange
1/2	teaspoon ground nutmeg		4	tablespoons melted butter
1	teaspoon vanilla extract			
12	cups panettone, cut into 1-inch cubes (Italian holiday bread)			

In a large bowl, whisk eggs and half-and-half together until frothy. Whisk in the sugar, nutmeg and vanilla extract. Stir in panettone, cranberries, pecans, orange zest and juice and melted butter. Pour into a greased 9×13×3-inch baking pan. Cover with foil. (Can be made a day ahead.) Bake in preheated 350-degree oven for 1 hour. Remove foil, bake an additional 15 minutes until center is set and pudding is puffed and golden. Remove from oven. Cool slightly before cutting. Cut into 2×2-inch pieces and serve with rum sauce on top.

Serves at least 12

Note: This recipe is very rich, so go light on the serving pieces.

Rum Sauce

1	stick (4 ounces) butter		1/8	teaspoon salt
1	cup heavy cream		1/4	cup dark rum
1	cup light brown sugar		1/4	teaspoon ground nutmeg

In a medium saucepan, heat the butter until melted. Whisk in the cream, brown sugar, salt, rum and nutmeg. Simmer on low for 5 minutes until sugar is melted. Taste for seasoning. Refrigerate until ready to use, then reheat.

Makes about 1 1/2 cups sauce

Note: Can be made a day ahead.

Kahlúa-Scented Chocolate Bread Pudding with Bourbon Sauce

10 large eggs
1   cup sugar
1   tablespoon vanilla extract
1   cup chocolate chips, melted
1   quart half-and-half
1   pound hearty bread such as Italian, challah or French country, cut into cubes (at least 8 cups)

1/4 cup Kahlúa (coffee liqueur)
1/2 cup chopped pecans, walnuts or macadamia nuts
2   tablespoons melted butter

In a large bowl, combine eggs, sugar and vanilla. Whisk until eggs are frothy. Melt the chocolate chips in a bowl over a pot of simmering water (double boiler). Whisk the melted chocolate and the half-and-half together. Add to egg mixture. Add bread, Kahlúa and nuts. Mix well. Spread the melted butter in a 9×13-inch baking pan. Pour the bread mixture into pan. Spread evenly. Cover loosely with foil. Bake on middle rack of 350-degree oven for 1 hour. Uncover and bake an additional 15 minutes until puffed and center is set. Cool. Cut into 9 pieces. Serve with bourbon sauce.

Serves 9

Bourbon Sauce

1/2 stick (2 ounces) butter
2   cups powdered sugar
1/4 cup bourbon

1   teaspoon vanilla extract
    zest and juice of 1 orange

In a medium saucepan, heat butter. On low heat, slowly whisk in the powdered sugar. Take the pan off the heat, add the bourbon, vanilla, orange zest and juice. Return to heat and whisk on low heat for 1 minute. Serve sauce warm over bread pudding.

Makes about 1 cup

Ricotta Cream Filling

1 pound whole-milk ricotta	2 tablespoons chopped lemon or
1/3 cup sugar or 1/2 cup powdered sugar	orange citron (or 1 tablespoon
drop of cinnamon oil (use sparingly)	orange marmalade)
zest of 1 orange	1/4 cup mini chocolate chips

Beat ricotta and sugar together in mixing bowl until smooth, about 2 minutes. Beat in cinnamon oil for 1 minute. Stir in orange zest, citron and chocolate chips. Use in Sicilian Cassata (recipe follows), stuff 24 small cream puff shells or to fill 12 cannoli shells.

Sicilian Cassata

24-inch piece of plastic wrap	1/4 cup dark rum
1 pound loaf pound cake, cut into	1 cup heavy cream
4 slices, horizontally or three 8-inch	1/2 cup powdered sugar
sponge cakes, 1/2 inch thick	1 teaspoon vanilla extract
1/4 cup orange liqueur (Triple Sec,	1 pint strawberries, sliced
Cointreau, Grand Marnier) or	
1/4 cup cherry liqueur (Kirsch)	

Line a 1-pound loaf pan with plastic wrap, allowing enough overhang so cake can be wrapped completely when assembled. Place bottom layer of pound cake in the loaf pan. Combine the liqueur and rum in small bowl and brush the cake with 1/4 of the liquid. Spread 1/3 of the ricotta filling over cake, top with another slice of pound cake, brush with 1/4 more of the liqueur mixture, and continue with the layering process until top layer of cake is brushed with liqueur. Wrap the plastic around the cake and refrigerate at least 4 hours and up to 24 hours. When ready to serve cake, beat heavy cream with powdered sugar and vanilla extract until stiff. Remove cake from plastic wrap, place on serving platter and spread whipped cream over top and sides evenly. Place sliced strawberries around the perimeter of cake and serve in 1-inch thick slices.

Serves 8

For use with sponge cake: Place one layer of 8-inch sponge cake in a plastic-lined 9-inch springform pan. Brush with liqueur mixture, spread 1/2 of the ricotta filling over cake, top with another cake, brush with liqueur, spread with remaining 1/2 of ricotta filling, cake, liqueur and wrap in plastic and place in refrigerator for at least 4 hours and up to 24 hours. When ready to serve cake, beat heavy cream with powdered sugar and vanilla extract until stiff. Remove cake from plastic wrap, place on serving platter and spread whipped cream over top and sides evenly. Place sliced strawberries around perimeter of cake and cut into 10 wedges.

Serves 10

Decadent Chocolate Cheesecake

Crust

1 1/2 cups chocolate wafer crumbs
1/2 cup ground almonds

4 tablespoons melted butter

Combine the chocolate wafer crumbs, almonds and melted butter in a bowl. Mix well. Press into the bottom of a 9-inch springform pan. Bake in a preheated 350-degree oven for 10 minutes; cool.

Filling

4 (8-ounce) packages (2 pounds) cream cheese, softened
1 cup sugar
1/3 cup powdered cocoa
4 large eggs

1 cup sour cream
1 tablespoon vanilla extract
1 teaspoon almond extract
2 cups freshly sliced strawberries or raspberries

In a mixer bowl, beat the cream cheese, sugar, cocoa, eggs, sour cream, vanilla extract and almond extract until well blended, about 3 minutes on medium speed. Pour into prepared springform pan. Bake in a 425-degree oven for 15 minutes, reduce heat to 300 degrees and bake for an additional 50 to 60 minutes, until center is set. Remove from oven. Cool to room temperature, refrigerate until ready to serve. Remove outer ring from pan. Serve with freshly sliced strawberries or raspberries on the side.

Serves 12 to 16

New York-Style Lemon Cheesecake

Crust

1 1/2 cups graham cracker crumbs
1/4 cup finely ground almonds
1/2 teaspoon cinnamon
4 tablespoons melted butter

Combine all ingredients and press evenly into the bottom of a 9-inch springform pan. Set aside.

Filling

1 1/2 pounds (24 ounces) cream cheese, softened
1 pint (16 ounces) sour cream
1 tablespoon cornstarch
3 large eggs
1 cup sugar
1 teaspoon vanilla extract
1 tablespoon finely grated lemon zest
1/4 teaspoon salt

In a mixer bowl, beat the cream cheese and sour cream until smooth. Add the cornstarch, eggs, sugar, vanilla, lemon zest and salt. Beat for 2 minutes on medium speed. Pour into the prepared springform pan. Bake in a preheated 425-degree oven for 15 minutes, then reduce heat to 325 degrees and bake an additional 60 minutes. Carefully remove from oven. Cool to room temperature, then refrigerate for at least 8 hours before removing outer rim of pan.

Serves 12 to 16

Note: Love New York cheesecake? This is the best . . . rich, lemon-scented and satisfying. Serve it alone or with freshly sliced strawberries or raspberries. Best made a day or two ahead then refrigerated. This cake also freezes well. It is a must have on our Thanksgiving table.

Pumpkin Spiced Cheesecake

Crust

20   gingersnap cookies
1/4   cup chopped walnuts

3   tablespoons butter, melted

In a food processor, grind the gingersnaps and walnuts. Remove to a bowl, add the melted butter and mix well. Press into the bottom of a 10-inch springform pan.

Filling

5   (8-ounce) packages (2 1/2 pounds) cream cheese, softened
1 1/4 cups brown sugar
5   large eggs
2   large egg yolks
2   cups pumpkin purée
1/3   cup evaporated milk

1/4   cup flour
2   teaspoons vanilla extract
1   teaspoon cinnamon
1   teaspoon ground cloves
1   teaspoon ground ginger
1/4   teaspoon ground nutmeg
1/4   teaspoon ground allspice

In a mixer bowl, beat the cream cheese, brown sugar, eggs, egg yolks, pumpkin purée, evaporated milk, flour, vanilla extract, cinnamon, cloves, ginger, nutmeg and allspice. Beat for about 3 minutes until all ingredients are well blended. Pour into prepared springform pan. Bake in 425-degree oven for 15 minutes, reduce heat to 325 degrees and bake for an additional hour and 20 minutes. Center should be set. Transfer to rack and cool completely. Refrigerate for at least 8 hours before serving.

Topping

1   cup heavy cream
1/4   cup powdered sugar

1   teaspoon vanilla extract
     ground nutmeg

For topping, beat the heavy cream with powdered sugar and vanilla extract until stiff peaks form. Top each slice of cheesecake with a dollop of cream and sprinkle with a little nutmeg.

Serves 16 to 20

Apple and Cranberry Sour Cream Cobbler

Filling

8	large Granny Smith or Pippin apples, peeled, cored and sliced thin (8 cups)	1	teaspoon ground cinnamon
		1/2	teaspoon ground nutmeg
		1/2	teaspoon ground ginger
1	(12-ounce) bag fresh cranberries	3/4	cup sugar
1	cup raisins	1/4	cup brown sugar
	zest and juice of 1 orange		16 ounces (1 pint) sour cream

In a bowl, combine the apples, cranberries, raisins, orange zest and juice, cinnamon, nutmeg, ginger, sugar, brown sugar and sour cream. Stir to combine well. Pour into a 2-quart baking pan.

Cobbler Crust

3	cups flour	1	teaspoon salt
1	stick (4 ounces) cold butter, cut into 8 pieces	1	teaspoon baking powder
		1	to 1 1/2 cups half-and-half
1	tablespoon sugar	2	tablespoons sugar (topping)

In a bowl, combine the flour and butter with a pastry cutter or crumble with your fingers. Add the 1 tablespoon sugar, salt, baking powder and enough half-and-half to make a soft dough. Place the dough mixture in dollops on the apple filling, spreading as you go. Don't make it perfect. It should look rustic (cobblers are not works of art). Sprinkle with the 2 tablespoons sugar and bake in a 375-degree oven for 45 minutes or until dough is golden and filling is bubbly.

Topping

1	quart best-quality vanilla ice cream or 2 cups whipped cream

Remove cobbler from oven, cool slightly and serve with a scoop of vanilla ice cream or whipped cream on top. Dust with a little cinnamon or nutmeg, if desired.

Serves 8 to 10

Apple Blueberry Crisp

Filling

6   large cooking apples such as Granny Smith or Pippins, peeled, cored and sliced thin

2   cups blueberries, fresh or thawed, if frozen

zest and juice of 1 large lemon

3/4   cup sugar

In a medium bowl, combine the apple slices, blueberries, lemon zest and juice and sugar. Toss well. Pour in a 9×13-inch baking dish.

Topping

1   cup flour
1   cup uncooked oats
1   teaspoon cinnamon
1/4   teaspoon nutmeg
1/2   cup brown sugar

1   cup coarsely chopped pecans
6   tablespoons cold butter, cut into 6 pieces
whipped cream or vanilla ice cream

In a bowl, combine the flour, oats, cinnamon, nutmeg, brown sugar and pecans. Cut the cold butter pieces into the mixture with a pastry cutter or a fork until butter is "pea-sized." Sprinkle evenly over apple filling. Bake in a preheated 400-degree oven for 30 minutes until apples are cooked and topping is golden brown. Serve warm with whipped cream or vanilla ice cream.

Serves 8

Note: This is a perfect summer dessert when made with fresh peaches. Substitute 6 large peaches, pitted and sliced, for the apples. Follow the recipe as given.

Orange Flan

1	cup plus 2 tablespoons sugar	6	large egg yolks
	zest of 1 orange	4	large whole eggs
1	cup heavy cream	1/4	cup honey
2	cups whole milk		

Place 1 cup sugar in heavy saucepan and cook on medium heat until golden brown and forms caramel. This process takes about 3 to 4 minutes. The sugar will turn liquid and brown very fast after the first 3 minutes. Carefully pour caramel into a 10-inch Pyrex pie plate. Quickly tilt plate so that the caramel is an even layer on the bottom of plate. Add the zest of 1 orange, cream and milk in same saucepan as you cooked the caramel. Bring to a simmer over medium heat. Turn off heat. In a medium bowl, beat the egg yolks, whole eggs and honey until frothy. Add the 2 tablespoons remaining sugar. Temper the eggs by whisking 1/2 cup of the scaled milk to eggs, then pour in remaining cream and milk mixture and whisk well. Pour into caramel-lined pie plate and place pie plate in a baking pan large enough so you can add hot tap water to pan to go halfway up the side of the pie plate to make a "Bain Marie." Cover pie plate loosely with foil. Bake on center rack of a preheated 325-degree oven for 1 1/2 hours or until knife inserted in center comes out clean. Allow to cool 1 hour before chilling. Refrigerate overnight or at least 8 hours. When ready to serve, run a sharp knife around edge of flan and invert onto another platter. Serve with fresh fruit, whipped cream or orange slices.

Serves 8

Warmed Peach Melba and Ice Cream

2	tablespoons butter	2	peaches, pits removed, sliced into one-eighths
1/4	teaspoon cinnamon		
1/4	teaspoon ground nutmeg	1	pint fresh raspberries
2	tablespoons sugar	4	large scoops vanilla ice cream
	juice of 1 orange or lemon	4	fresh mint sprigs

In medium saucepan, heat butter. Add cinnamon, nutmeg, sugar, orange or lemon juice and peaches. Cook on low heat, stirring often for 2 minutes or until peaches are heated through. Remove from heat. Gently stir in raspberries. Place one scoop ice cream in serving bowl. Top with 1/4 of the mixture. Serve with fresh mint sprigs.

Serves 4

*Note: When peaches and raspberries are in season, this is the perfect summer dessert.
Try it with peach or raspberry ice cream, or layer the peach and raspberry mixture
in between sweetened mascarpone cheese in a parfait glass and topped with chopped
amaretti cookies or chopped toasted almonds. Deliciously refreshing!*

Panna Cotta

This is a light, yet satisfying dessert after a summer or winter meal.
Panna cotta, translated means "cooked cream."

2	cups heavy cream	1/2	cup sugar
1	envelope unflavored gelatin	2	teaspoons vanilla extract or
1/4	cup whole milk		1 teaspoon lemon extract
8	ounces sour cream		vegetable spray

Place cream in a medium saucepan. Heat on low until warmed through, about 3 minutes. Place gelatin in a small bowl with whole milk and allow to soften for 5 minutes, stirring often. Whisk the gelatin, sour cream, sugar and extract into warmed milk. Whisk well until the gelatin and sugar dissolve. Pour the mixture into a 4-cup mold which has been sprayed with vegetable oil or use six 5-ounce ramekins, also sprayed with vegetable oil. Refrigerate at least 4 hours to allow the panna cotta to set. Unmold onto a serving platter and surround the panna cotta with fruit of choice.

Serves 6 to 8

Spring and Summer Fruit

1	pint raspberries	2	tablespoons sugar
1	pint blackberries, blueberries or huckleberries	1	tablespoon Kirsch (cherry liqueur), optional
1	pint strawberries, hulled and quartered		

Combine all ingredients in a bowl. Refrigerate until ready to use.

Makes about 4 cups

Note: You can use any fresh fruit in season, such as sliced peaches, nectarines, mangoes, papayas, kiwi or even apricots. Use what you like, is fresh and flavorful.

Autumn and Winter Fruit

1/2	cup golden raisins		zest and juice of 1 large orange
1/2	cup dark raisins	1/4	cup dark rum
1/2	cup sun-dried cranberries or sun-dried cherries	1/2	cup honey

Combine all ingredients in a small saucepan. Simmer on low heat for 5 minutes. Refrigerate until ready to use, then reheat slightly before serving.

Makes about 2 cups

Grandma Rose's Rice Pudding

2	quarts whole milk			pinch of salt
1/4	teaspoon lemon zest		3	large eggs
3/4	cup converted long grain rice		1	teaspoon vanilla extract
1/2	cup sugar			cinnamon
1	teaspoon butter			

In a large saucepan, bring the milk, lemon zest, rice, sugar, butter and salt to a simmer. Cook for 30 minutes on low heat, stirring occasionally, making sure the rice does not stick to the bottom of the pan. Taste the rice after 30 minutes. It should be tender.

In a large bowl, beat the eggs and vanilla extract until frothy. Slowly stir 2/3 of the hot rice into the egg mixture. Return the rice and eggs to the saucepan with remaining rice and on low heat, stir the rice constantly for 5 to 8 minutes until creamy. Pour into a 2-quart shallow dish, sprinkle with cinnamon and refrigerate until ready to serve.

Serves 8 to 10

Tarte Tatin

2	tablespoons butter	1	sheet store-bought frozen puff
1/2	cup sugar		pastry, thawed and rolled out
4	large Granny Smith apples, peeled, cored and thinly sliced		vanilla ice cream or whipped cream

In an 8-inch ovenproof skillet, (cast-iron works best), heat butter and sugar and cook on medium heat for 2 or 3 minutes until sugar is caramelized. Watch this process carefully for the sugar will caramelize quickly. Place the sliced apples on caramel in decorative manner, being careful not to burn your fingers. Cut the pastry sheet into an 8-inch diameter circle. Place pastry on top of apples, bake in 425-degree oven for 25 minutes or until golden brown. Remove from oven; cool slightly and carefully invert the tart onto a serving platter. Cut into 6 wedges and serve with vanilla ice cream or whipped cream.

Serves 6

Note: This is an easy dessert with only 4 ingredients. Allow the tart to cool slightly before inverting, lifting the apples on the bottom with a spatula to insure the apples are not sticking to pan. Make sure you use a cooking apple such as Granny Smith or Pippin, for others will be too juicy and make the tart soggy. Perfect dessert in the fall with a pork entrée.

Tiramisu

"Tiramisu" in Italian means "lift me up" and with the booze, it does that!

36	ladyfinger cookies or 18 soft ladyfingers that are doubled (divide in half for 36 pieces)	1	cup heavy cream
		1/4	cup sugar
2	cups strong espresso coffee	2	tablespoons dark rum
1/4	cup Kahlúa (coffee-flavored liqueur)	1	pint fresh raspberries (optional)
2	tablespoons sugar	1	tablespoon cocoa powder
1	pound mascarpone cheese (Italian cream cheese)		

Place 12 ladyfingers on the bottom of a decorative 8-inch round dish at least 4 inches deep. Combine the coffee, Kahlúa and 2 tablespoons sugar in a small bowl. Brush the ladyfingers with 1/3 of the coffee mixture. They should be fairly moist.

In a mixer bowl, beat the mascarpone with heavy cream, 1/4 cup sugar and rum until thick, about 1 minute on medium speed. Spread 1/3 of the cream mixture on top of ladyfingers. Sprinkle with 1/3 of the raspberries. Top with 12 more ladyfingers, 1/3 of the coffee mixture, 1/3 of the cream, 1/3 of berries, and continue with third layer, finishing with berries. Sprinkle with cocoa powder, cover loosely and refrigerate for at least 2 hours and up to 24 hours before serving. Serve small portions, it is very rich!!

Serves 8 to 10

Note: You can eliminate the raspberries when they are not in season. Tiramisu is traditionally served without fruit, but I like the look and taste of the berries in summer.

Chocolate Almond Torte

Cake Layers

6   large egg whites
      pinch of cream of tartar
1/4 cup sugar
6   large egg yolks
1/2 cup sugar
1/2 teaspoon baking powder

1/2 teaspoon almond extract
1/4 cup flour
1/2 cup finely chopped semisweet
      chocolate
1/2 cup finely chopped almonds

In a mixer bowl, beat egg whites with cream of tartar and 1/4 cup sugar until stiff peaks form. Set aside.

Beat the egg yolks with 1/2 cup sugar until light and lemon colored. Beat in the baking powder, almond extract, flour, chocolate and almonds. Carefully fold the beaten egg whites into the yolk mixture. Pour the batter into two 8-inch round cake pans which have been greased and lined with parchment or waxed paper cut out to fit bottom of pans. Bake in a 350-degree oven for 25 minutes. Remove from oven, cool to room temperature and then turn out onto cake racks. Peel the paper from bottom of the cakes. Allow to cool completely before filling the layers.

Filling

2   cups heavy cream
1   teaspoon vanilla extract

1/2 cup powdered sugar

Whip heavy cream with vanilla and powdered sugar until stiff peaks form. Place a cake layer on a cake plate, top with 1/3 of the whipped cream, place second cake layer on top of cream, spread remaining cream on top and sides of cake.

Garnish

chocolate shavings or chocolate leaves

fresh strawberry halves
1/2 cup toasted almond slices

Garnish with your choice of chocolate shavings, chocolate leaves, strawberry halves and/or almond slices. Refrigerate the cake for at least 2 hours (and up to 24) before cutting.

Serves 8 to 10

Pine Nut Torta

This is a very traditional Sicilian dessert. Not too sweet, it makes a perfect ending to any meal.

1   piecrust or puff pastry large enough to fit a 9-inch fluted pan with
      removable bottom

Press piecrust into fluted tart pan, coming up the sides, or use a traditional 9-inch pie pan and flute the edges.

Filling

2	cups (1 pound) ricotta cheese		grated zest of 1 lemon
1/2	cup half-and-half		grated zest of 1 orange
2	large eggs	1/2	cup toasted pine nuts (place in
1	egg yolk		350-degree oven for 5 minutes
1/3	cup sugar		to toast)

In a medium bowl, whisk together all ingredients for filling. Pour into prepared pie shell. Place on a baking sheet. Bake at 375 degrees for 30 minutes or until golden and filling is set. Cool thoroughly.

Garnish

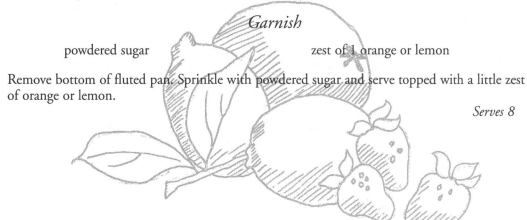

powdered sugar   zest of 1 orange or lemon

Remove bottom of fluted pan. Sprinkle with powdered sugar and serve topped with a little zest of orange or lemon.

Serves 8

Old-Fashioned Carrot Cake

3 large eggs
2 cups flour
2 cups sugar
1 1/4 cups vegetable or canola oil
2 teaspoons baking soda
1 teaspoon cinnamon
1/2 teaspoon ground cloves

1/2 teaspoon nutmeg
1 teaspoon salt
2 teaspoons vanilla extract
1 cup shredded sweetened coconut
1 cup chopped walnuts
1 cup crushed pineapple, drained
2 cups shredded raw carrots

In a mixer bowl, beat the eggs until foamy and then slowly add the flour, sugar, oil, baking soda, cinnamon, cloves, nutmeg, salt and vanilla extract. Beat until smooth. Stir in the coconut, walnuts, pineapple and carrots until well combined. Pour into a greased and floured 9×13×3-inch baking pan. Bake in a preheated 350-degree oven for 50 to 55 minutes. Remove from oven; cool. Spread the top of cake with Orange Cream Cheese Frosting.

Serves 12

Orange Cream Cheese Frosting

4 tablespoons (1/2 stick) butter, softened
8 ounces cream cheese, softened

2 cups powdered sugar
1 teaspoon vanilla extract
zest and juice of 1 large orange

In a medium bowl, beat the butter, cream cheese, powdered sugar, vanilla extract and orange zest and juice until smooth. Use as a frosting on carrot cake.

Note: This is a recipe my mother used to make for birthdays, picnics and summer dinners on the patio. It is moist, has all the wonderful spices of a great carrot cake and the orange frosting is the perfect topping to it all. For carrot cake lovers, look no further!

Chocolate Mousse Cake

Crust

3 cups chocolate wafer crumbs

¹/₂ cup (1 stick) butter, melted

Combine crumbs and butter and press onto bottom and sides of 10-inch springform pan. Refrigerate 30 minutes.

Filling

1 pound semisweet chocolate chips
2 large eggs
4 large egg yolks

2 cups heavy cream
¹/₃ cup powdered sugar
4 large egg whites

In the top of a double boiler over simmering water, melt chocolate. Allow to cool slightly and whip in the 2 large eggs and 4 large egg yolks. Whip the heavy cream with powdered sugar until stiff peaks form. In another clean bowl, whip the egg whites until stiff peaks form. Fold the cream into chocolate mixture and then fold egg whites into chocolate mixture until well incorporated. Do not overmix. Turn into crust and chill at least 6 hours or overnight.

Topping

1 cup heavy cream
¹/₄ cup powdered sugar
1 teaspoon vanilla extract

6 whole strawberries, hulled, cut in half

When ready to serve, beat heavy cream, powdered sugar and vanilla extract until stiff peaks form. Loosen crust on all sides using sharp knife. Remove outer rim of pan. Spread whipped cream over the top of the cake or pipe rosettes around cake. Place 12 strawberry halves around the edge of the cake. Cut the cake with a wet sharp knife.

Serves 12

Girl Scout Thin Mint and White Chocolate Mousse Brownie Cake

1   package brownie mix (enough for one 8×8-inch pan)
1   envelope unflavored gelatin
1/2 cup half-and-half
1   cup white chocolate morsels
2   cups heavy whipping cream

1/2 cup powdered sugar
18 Girl Scout Thin Mint cookies, coarsely crushed in food processor
6   large strawberries, cut in half lengthwise

Make brownie mix according to package directions and pour into a 10-inch springform pan. Bake at 325 degrees for 25 minutes. Brownie base will be soft. Remove from oven and cool in refrigerator for 15 minutes while making filling.

Place gelatin and half-and-half in small saucepan. Allow to soften for 5 minutes. Heat on low and stir for 2 minutes until gelatin is melted. Remove from heat.

Place white chocolate morsels in a glass bowl, cover with plastic wrap and melt on low in microwave for 1 minute. They should be slightly softened.

Pour heavy cream in mixer bowl of electric mixer. Beat on medium speed until soft peaks form, add powdered sugar, softened white chocolate morsels and gelatin mixture. Beat on medium speed until stiff peaks form, about another minute. Fold in the crushed Girl Scout Thin Mint cookies. Pour filling into pan with brownie base. Refrigerate for at least 4 hours and up to 24 hours. Remove outer ring from springform pan using a warmed knife to loosen cake from the ring. Garnish outer edge of cake with 12 strawberry halves.

Serves 12

Note: This is a recipe I developed for the Girl Scouts of America for their cookie "promotion week." Rich, decadent and it uses their number one seller, Thin Mint Cookies.

Italian Cheese Pie

Crust

2	cups flour		1	large egg
1/4	teaspoon salt		2	tablespoons sherry, Marsala or
1/4	cup sugar			vinegar
4	ounces (1 stick) butter			about 1/2 cup iced water

In a food processor, combine the flour, salt, sugar, butter and egg. Pulse on and off until dough is coarse. Slowly add the sherry and the iced water, a tablespoon at a time, pulsing on and off until dough forms a soft ball. Do not overprocess for it will make a tough dough. Form 2 balls. Roll out one ball onto a floured work surface to a 10-inch diameter circle. Place in a deep 9-inch pie pan, crimp edges and set aside. Roll out remaining dough to a 10-inch diameter circle and cut into twelve 1/2-inch wide strips. This will form a "lattice" over the pie.

Filling

1 1/2	pounds whole-milk ricotta		1	tablespoon vanilla extract
1/4	cup toasted chopped almonds		4	large eggs
1	tablespoon orange zest		1/3	cup sugar
1	tablespoon lemon zest		1/4	teaspoon salt

Egg Wash

1   egg beaten with 1 tablespoon cream

In a mixer bowl, combine the ricotta, almonds, orange zest, lemon zest, vanilla extract, eggs, sugar and salt. Beat for 1 minute on medium speed. Pour into prepared piecrust. Loosely place 6 strips of dough in one direction on top of pie. Then place 6 strips in opposite direction to form a "lattice" on top of pie. Crimp edges of lattice with the bottom layer of piecrust. Brush with egg wash. Bake in preheated 350-degree oven for 1 hour until filling is firm and pastry is golden brown. Remove from oven; cool to room temperature and sprinkle with powdered sugar before serving.

Serves 8 to 10

Note: This pie tastes best if made a day ahead, then refrigerated. This is a traditional Easter dessert served in Italy with variations from region to region.
It is a favorite at my house as it was at my mother's.

Sour Cream Apple Walnut Pie

Crust

Crust for one 9-inch pie

Place crust in a 9-inch pie pan. Crimp edges. Set aside.

Filling

6	large cooking apples such as Granny Smith or Pippin, peeled, cored, sliced	1	large egg, beaten
1	cup sour cream	1/4	teaspoon salt
1/3	cup sugar	1	teaspoon vanilla extract
		1/4	cup flour
			zest and juice of 1 lemon

Have the apples peeled, cored and sliced in a separate bowl. In a medium bowl, combine the sour cream, sugar, beaten egg, salt, vanilla extract, flour, lemon zest and juice. Toss in the apple slices. Pour into prepared pie shell.

Topping

1/4	cup brown sugar	1	cup chopped walnuts
1/4	cup sugar		whipped cream or vanilla ice cream
1	teaspoon cinnamon		

In a small bowl, combine the brown sugar, sugar, cinnamon and walnuts. Spread evenly over the apple filling. Bake in a preheated 350-degree oven for 55 to 60 minutes or until bubbly. Serve warm with whipped cream or vanilla ice cream.

Serves 8

Southern Pecan Pie

4 large eggs
1 cup sugar
1/4 teaspoon salt
1 cup light corn syrup
2 teaspoons flour
1 teaspoon vanilla extract

1 cup pecan pieces
1 cup pecan halves
1/4 cup (1/2 stick) butter, melted
2 tablespoons bourbon
1 unbaked (9-inch) pie shell

In a medium bowl, beat eggs with mixer until well blended. Beat in sugar, salt, corn syrup, flour and vanilla for 1 minute on medium speed. Stir in pecans, butter and bourbon. Pour filling into prepared pie shell. Bake on middle shelf of preheated 350-degree oven for 55 minutes. Cool to room temperature and serve with whipped cream if desired.

Serves 8

Warm Cinnamon Apple Tart

2 tablespoons sugar
1 teaspoon ground cinnamon
1 sheet store-bought frozen puff pastry, thawed
1 egg, beaten to blend (for glaze)

1/4 cup apricot preserves
2 tablespoons lemon juice
1 tablespoon butter
2 Golden Delicious apples, peeled, cored and sliced very thin

Combine sugar and cinnamon in small bowl. Place pastry on baking sheet. Brush some of the egg glaze over 1-inch outer border of pastry. With a sharp knife, score the 1-inch border in a crisscross pattern. Heat apricot preserves with lemon juice and butter in a small saucepan.

Brush pastry (not the border) with thin layer of preserves. Lay the apple slices on pastry in 3 even rows, overlapping apples and leaving the 1-inch border. Sprinkle with sugar-cinnamon mixture. Bake in 400-degree oven for 25 minutes. Remove from oven, brush with remaining warmed apricot mixture. Serve warm with vanilla ice cream.

Serves 4

Note: Try this tart substituting fresh peaches for the apples in summer. Use about 3 large peaches, thinly sliced and sprinkled with a few fresh blueberries.

Apple Cranberry Tart

Pastry for one 10-inch piecrust
zest and juice of 1 large orange
2 Granny Smith or Pippin apples, peeled, cored and grated
1 cup fresh cranberries
1/2 cup raisins
1 cup sugar
1/2 cup brown sugar
1 tablespoon instant tapioca
1/2 teaspoon cinnamon
1/8 teaspoon ground cloves
1/4 cup chopped walnuts
whipped cream, optional

Place the piecrust in a 9-inch tart pan with a removable bottom.

In a medium bowl, combine the orange zest, orange juice, grated apples, cranberries, raisins, sugar, brown sugar, tapioca, cinnamon and cloves. Toss well. Place in the prepared piecrust. Sprinkle on the chopped walnuts. Bake on a foil-lined baking sheet (to catch any drippings) in a preheated 400-degree oven for 15 minutes, reduce heat to 350 degrees and bake an additional 30 minutes. Allow to cool to room temperature before removing outer rim. Serve with whipped cream, if desired.

Serves 8

Note: This is one of my favorite autumn desserts . . . perfect for your holiday table or just with a cup of coffee or tea on a Sunday afternoon.

Lemon Almond Tart

Piecrust

2	cups flour		1	tablespoon sugar
4	ounces (1 stick) butter, cut into 8 pieces		1/4	teaspoon salt
4	tablespoons vegetable shortening		1/4	to 1/2 cup iced water

In food processor, place flour, butter, shortening, sugar and salt. Pulse on and off until dough is size of peas. Slowly, with motor running, add enough iced water to form a moist ball. Do not overwork the dough. Remove from work bowl and knead on floured work surface into a ball, refrigerate 30 minutes. Roll out dough to a 12-inch diameter circle. Press dough into a 10-inch tart pan with removable bottom. Cut away excess dough. Set aside.

Filling

3	large eggs		5	tablespoons butter, melted
3/4	cup sugar		1/2	teaspoon vanilla extract
8	tablespoons fresh lemon juice		1	cup ground almonds
1	tablespoon grated lemon zest			

In a medium bowl, beat the eggs and sugar until frothy and lemon colored. Beat in lemon juice and lemon zest. Gradually pour in the melted butter, vanilla extract and ground almonds. Beat until well combined and pour into prepared tart shell. Bake in preheated 350-degree oven for 30 minutes or until filling is set. Allow the tart to cool to room temperature before removing outer ring of tart pan. Sprinkle with powdered sugar and cut into 8 wedges.

Serves 8

Almond Biscotti

4	ounces (1 stick) butter, softened	1	teaspoon baking powder
1¹/₂	cups sugar	1	teaspoon vanilla extract
4	large eggs	1	teaspoon almond extract
4	cups flour	2	cups chopped toasted almonds

In a mixer bowl, cream the butter and sugar until fluffy and a light lemon color, about 2 minutes on medium speed. Add the eggs, one at a time, while beating on low speed. Gradually add the flour, baking powder, vanilla extract, almond extract and almonds. Grease a baking sheet. Divide the dough into 2 equal pieces and roll each piece into a log 2 inches in diameter, 1 inch in height and about 15 inches long. Place logs on baking sheet. Bake in a 375-degree oven for 12 to 15 minutes or until golden brown on top and sides, but don't cook the dough through. They should be slightly underdone in the center. Remove from oven, cool 5 minutes and then cut the dough on a diagonal into 1-inch wide slices. Place cookie slices back on the baking sheet on their sides and return to oven for 5 to 7 more minutes until golden and crispy. Remove from oven, cool to room temperature and store the biscotti in an airtight container or ziplock bags.

Makes about 36 cookies

Almond Spritz Cookies

1	cup (2 sticks) butter, softened	¹/₂	teaspoon baking powder
1	cup sugar	¹/₄	teaspoon salt
1	large egg		colored candy sprinkles
1	teaspoon almond extract		candied cherry halves
2¹/₃	cups flour		colored sugars

In a mixer bowl, beat the butter and sugar until creamy. Add the egg, almond extract, flour, baking powder and salt and beat until dough is combined. Do not chill dough. Pack the dough, a small section at a time, into a cookie press. Press into desired shapes onto an ungreased cookie sheet. Sprinkle with desired toppings or you can add food coloring to the dough as you are mixing in the other ingredients. Bake at 400 degrees in middle of the oven for 7 minutes. Cool.

Makes about 5 dozen cookies

Note: I used to make dozens of cookies at Christmas with Justin and Sarah decorating
as we pressed the dough onto the cookie sheets, topping with cherry halves and colored candies.
The possibilities were endless and we would add green food coloring to the dough for the
"tree" shaped press. I think they ate as many as they decorated.

Butter Horns (Cinnamon Walnut Crescents)

Dough

8	ounces sour cream
2	cups all-purpose flour
1	large egg yolk

1/2	cup (1 stick) butter, softened
1/2	cup (1 stick) margarine, softened

In a mixer bowl, combine all ingredients until a soft ball forms. Divide dough into 2 pieces, wrap each piece in plastic wrap and refrigerate for 8 hours or overnight.

Filling

3/4	cup sugar
1/4	cup finely chopped walnuts

1	teaspoon ground cinnamon

Combine the sugar, walnuts and cinnamon in a small bowl.

Topping

1	cup powdered sugar

To make cookies: Take dough out of the refrigerator, cut each piece into thirds so you have 6 pieces. Flour work surface. Roll each piece into an 8-inch circle. Sprinkle each circle with 1/6 of the filling. Cut each circle into 10 wedges and roll from wide end to narrow end to form a "crescent." Place on baking sheet with pointed end down. You should have 60 pieces. Bake in a preheated 350-degree oven for 12 minutes or until golden brown. Remove from oven and sprinkle with powdered sugar.

Makes 60 cookies

Note: These freeze well.

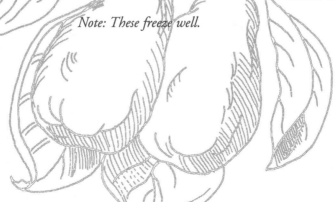

Italian Lemon Cookies

3¹/2 cups flour
2¹/2 teaspoons baking powder
3 large eggs
¹/2 cup sugar
4 ounces (1 stick) butter, softened
grated zest of 1 lemon

¹/2 cup whole milk
2 teaspoons vanilla extract
2 cups powdered sugar
3 or 4 tablespoons orange juice
colored candy sprinkles

In a small bowl, sift flour and baking powder together. In mixing bowl, beat the eggs with the sugar until light and lemon colored. Add the softened butter and lemon zest. Slowly beat in the flour mixture. Gradually add the milk and vanilla extract. Dough should be soft. Divide dough into 6 sections. Roll out each section into a rope ¹/2 inch wide. Cut into 3-inch pieces and twist each piece to form a loop. Place on a greased or parchment-lined baking sheet. Bake in a 350-degree oven for 10 to 12 minutes or until light brown. Remove from oven and cool. Combine the powdered sugar and enough orange juice to form a thin icing. Brush on top of cookies and sprinkle with colored candies.

Makes about 4 dozen cookies, depending on size and shape of cookie

Note: These are popular in Italy during the Easter and Christmas holidays.
Be as creative as your imagination takes you as to what shapes to create . . . snails, bunny
rabbits, S shapes, whatever strikes your fancy! You can always find these lemon
cookies in Italian pastry shops in Brooklyn.

Pecan Butter Balls

1 cup salted butter, softened
¹/2 cup powdered sugar
2 cups sifted all-purpose flour
¹/4 teaspoon baking powder

1 teaspoon vanilla extract
1 cup finely chopped pecans
2 cups powdered sugar

In a mixer bowl, cream the butter and ¹/2 cup powdered sugar until creamy, about 2 minutes on medium speed. Slowly add the flour, baking powder, vanilla extract and pecans while on low speed and beat for another minute. Dough should be soft. Shape dough into 1-inch balls and place on cookie sheets. Bake at 325 degrees for 15 minutes or until golden brown. While still warm, remove cookies from baking sheet with a spatula and roll in remaining powdered sugar until coated on all sides. Cool.

Makes about 3 dozen cookies

Italian Honey Balls (Struffoli or Pignoli)

A traditional holiday sweet in Italy

4	cups flour	6	large eggs
2	teaspoons vanilla extract	3	cups vegetable or peanut oil
2	teaspoons dark rum	3	cups honey
1/4	cup sugar	1/2	cup sugar
2	teaspoons baking powder		colored candy sprinkles
1/2	cup (4 ounces) butter	1/2	cup toasted pine nuts
	zest of 1 lemon or 1 orange		

In a mixer bowl, combine the flour, vanilla, rum, sugar, baking powder, butter and lemon zest. Beat until combined and add eggs, one at a time until dough is well mixed; about 2 more minutes of mixing. Remove dough from bowl. Divide the dough into eighths, and on a floured board roll each piece into a rope about 1/2 inch thick and 12 inches long. Cut each rope into 1/2-inch pieces and set aside in a bowl with a little flour (prevents the dough pieces from sticking together).

When all the dough has been cut, heat oil in a large pot (at least 4-quart pot). Test one piece of dough to see if oil is hot. Dough should sizzle then rise to top of oil. Add about 12 pieces at a time, when golden brown, remove with slotted spoon to a paper towel-lined bowl. Dough should be crispy on outside and soft in center. Continue to fry remaining pieces until all dough is cooked. Be careful frying in oil . . . if oil should foam, turn off heat immediately and allow to cool. Continue with new oil. Remove paper towels from bowl when finished.

Heat honey and sugar in saucepan until sugar is dissolved and mixture is bubbling. Pour hot honey mixture over the fried balls in bowl and immediately toss to coat the dough with the honey. Gently pour onto a serving platter and shape into a pyramid. Sprinkle with colored candy sprinkles and pine nuts, if desired. Can be made several days ahead.

Makes a pyramid about 10 inches high and 8 inches in diameter

Struffoli or Pignoli, as they are also known, can be found in every Italian pastry shop in New York around the Christmas season. There are as many recipes for this dessert as there are cooks, so comparing recipes is a common tradition. It is a holiday staple at my house and my children cannot have Christmas without a big plate of these gems on the table to nibble on all day long.

Index

*Savor
the
Memories* ·

Marguerite Marceau Henderson
1529 Hubbard Avenue
Salt Lake City, Utah 84105
1-801-582-9204
Email: margueriteh@attbi.com

Please send me _____ copies of *Savor the Memories* at $19.95 each $ _____

Utah residents add 6.60% sales tax $ _____

Postage and handling at $2.95 each $ _____

Total $ _____

Name _____

Address _____

City   State   Zip

Telephone _____

Method of Payment: [   ] VISA
                     [   ] Check payable to Savor the Memories or
                         Marguerite Marceau Henderson

Account Number   Expiration Date

Signature _____

Photocopies will be accepted.